Airline Games

by Roger James Newton

Table of Contents

To my wife, Susan, who has been hugely supportive throughout the writing process. Her suggestions to improve the descriptions of characters have been very helpful on many occasions.

About the Author

Roger James Newton was born in Stockport and attended Stockport Grammar School, followed by the University of Sheffield, where he graduated in Law in 1970. He then trained and practised as a Solicitor in the Greater Manchester area before choosing a career in Industry and Commerce. In the 1970s and 1980s, he worked in Engineering first with Rolls-Royce and later with Babcock International. The second half of his career was spent in the Food Manufacturing sector. This is Roger's second book, and it is loosely based on some of the real-life characters taken from his non-fiction work, Fasten Seatbelts - Stories of British Civil Aviation.

Chapter 1
The Spring of 1986

Sir John Cresswell was immaculately attired, as was always the case. This Monday morning, in the early part of May in 1986, he was wearing one of his many Saville Row-tailored three-piece suits. They were favoured because the elegant waistcoats facilitated the display of his impressive gold pocket watch and chain. He had travelled a long way from his pre-Second World War days as a trainee mechanic in West London. Unfortunately, one consequence of his success was that even the skilled tailoring was insufficient to disguise what had become a somewhat expanded waistline.

The Corporate Office of the Midlands & West Group Limited was situated on King Street in London's West End, and the picture windows of the Chairman's corner office afforded Sir John pleasing views across the adjacent St James's Square. This outlook would not last for long. Spring was here, and the Square's foliage was now bursting rapidly into glorious fresh green, obstructing vision and, so far, having a careless disregard for the increasingly worrying attentions of Central London pollution.

The Square was a quiet enclave from the West End whirl, but its relative peace this morning was disturbed by the sudden backfiring of a car exhaust. This sound sharply reminded Sir John of what had been a very different scene, just over two years previously. On 17 April 1984, there had been demonstrations in the Square, outside the then Libyan Embassy, against the dictatorial rule of President Muammar Gaddafi. Shots had been fired without warning from the Embassy, taking the life of PC Yvonne Fletcher, who had been part of the police presence controlling the demonstrators.

Being diagonally opposite to the Embassy building, Sir John's office had been commandeered by a heavily-armed, black combat-suited SAS squad. The SAS then installed tripods and trained a number of high-velocity guns on the windows of the Embassy. The siege had continued for eleven days before its eventual resolution. After regaining possession of his office, Sir John had later donated generously to Police Charities supporting the family of PC Fletcher – it was appropriate to do so, and it was a gesture which he could well afford.

All seemed to be reasonably normal this morning, although the week had not started well. In accordance with his usual routine, Sir John had spent the weekend at Bishop's Lake, his 500-acre Midlands Estate. He had left early in the morning, travelling down to London in the chauffeured Rolls-Royce Silver Spirit. The "Roller" was the property of the Midlands & West Group, the umbrella holding company for the large number of wide-ranging, mostly engineering, businesses which Sir John had ruthlessly assembled over the past forty years or so. It had been a true "rags to riches" story, which had seen him progress from being a penniless, poorly-educated, trainee motor mechanic in West London, to reaching the heights of becoming not only extremely wealthy, but also a Knight of the Realm.

Historically, Rolls-Royce Motors had always been deliberately tardy in revealing performance figures, stating that the power output of its cars was "adequate." Modern car technology was progressing rapidly, and Sir John had followed the subject with his mechanic's eye. He increasingly held the view that the word "barely" should now be inserted before "adequate." The manufacturer needed to pull its socks up. He would probably give Rolls-Royce Motors one more chance when the "Roller" was replaced in a year or so. It was necessary for that company to move with the times, as he believed he had done throughout his highly successful business career.

Upon reaching London this morning, a stop was made at Wimpole Street, where bad news had been received. Sir John's Consultant had advised that, due to deteriorating discs in his back, the choice was either a seriously intrusive operation, with no assurance as to outcome, or the permanent wearing of a surgical corset. What was certain was an end to one of Sir John's most cherished leisure activities; his role as Master of Fox Hounds for the hunt which was local to Bishop's Lake. Most disappointing because this position had given him profile and status in the local community, not to mention the joys of owning the stable of hunters which he had maintained over the past twenty years in memory of his beloved first wife, Laura, who had so loved horses. They would now, of course, mostly have to go. Sir John was not a man to let the grass grow.

Sir John, the eldest of four children, was born in Colnbrook to the west of London in 1917. Here, the Creswell family had lived in rented accommodation. Sir John's father had served in the British Army throughout the First World War, but had found little post-war appreciation, only monotonous factory work. He consoled what he considered to be his misfortunes in life by nightly large doses of London Pride ale, followed by whisky chasers; an alcohol excess which would eventually occasion his early death.

Sir John's mother had held the family together by working long hours as a cleaner. One of her assignments had been at West London Motors Limited, where she had got to know its proprietor, Ted Manning. She explained to Ted that the eldest of her four children had left school at age fourteen to join his father in the factory, having shown no apparent academic potential. However, the boy appeared to have a fascination with engines, how they operated to propel vehicles and what associated components were necessary for this purpose. Ted was persuaded to give the boy a chance and, in September 1932, John Cresswell started his apprenticeship as a trainee mechanic at West London Motors Limited.

The early years in the workshop were spent getting to know the fundamentals of engines and of car operating systems. Ted Manning both maintained and sold vehicles. As time had moved on, the young mechanic and car enthusiast would gravitate ever more frequently from the workshop in order to deputise for Ted in the Sales Department.

John Cresswell had then discovered a hitherto unknown talent, that of empathy, the essential quality required of a super salesman. He was able to enter the minds of prospective customers and then convince them that their dreams and desires would be met by the car that the company just happened to have on offer at the relevant time. As the number of second-hand cars passing through the showroom of West London Motors steadily increased, through John's salesmanship talents, this success was recognised by the prestigious award to the small company of a manufacturer's agency for the supply of new cars.

Chapter 2
Business Building

John Cresswell had also found love. The raven-haired, slim, strong-featured and highly intelligent Laura Manning, with her beautiful grey-green eyes, was two years his senior. Laura had had the benefits of a private education at a small local Independent School, for which Ted had just been able to scrape together the fees. Laura now ran her father's office with diligence and efficiency. She became aware of her increasing attraction towards this physically impressive young trainee mechanic, six feet tall and with a lean body honed by a successful short career as an amateur light heavyweight. He seemed to have a clear vision of where he wished to progress in life, together with the drive and determination to succeed. Whilst Ted might have harboured ambitions for his carefully-nurtured daughter to attract a more conventional, possibly professionally-qualified partner, he was certainly not going to stand in the way of her happiness.

The couple's courtship soon commenced. They frequently enjoyed dancing together, and they made numerous visits to London theatres and cinemas. In early 1937, the marriage of Laura Manning to John Cresswell, who had now become the Sales Manager of West London Motors Limited, was duly celebrated. Six months later, Ted Manning was dead, cruelly taken by a brain haemorrhage. John and a heartbroken Laura Cresswell, both still in their early twenties, were now the joint owners of the company.

Laura set about the task of improving her husband's very basic reading and writing abilities. She found a willing pupil who was keen to acquire the skills necessary to progress in business and to ascend to the higher levels of Society. In their leisure moments, Laura had also taught her husband the rudiments of Chess. She found that she was playing against an individual who showed immediate talents for the game taking a wide view and thinking strategically. John would never take up the game of Chess seriously, but these mental abilities would clearly be invaluable assets for a future business career.

Subject to the constraints of a well-run back office, Laura decided to give John reasonably free rein in developing the business. Apart from car servicing and sales, John quickly appreciated there was also money to be made in producing and trading in motor components, including connectors, fastenings and control systems. Within a short time, West London Motors Limited had evolved to become the wider-based Western Engineering Limited.

Also, with Laura's encouragement, John had taken up flying lessons at the West London Flying Club at White Waltham in Berkshire. Here he had spent many hours in the hangars closely examining their occupants and acquainting himself with their engines, control systems and the large number of parts, rods, cables, wires, fasteners and connectors, which were essential in order to make aircraft work efficiently and safely. Twelve months later, Western Engineering Limited had established a subsidiary company sourcing and manufacturing aircraft parts.

John and Laura were now also seeking to acquire other companies in the same field. The British Government had belatedly woken up to the Nazi threat in Europe, and there was a major thrust to replace the RAF's antiquated fighter biplanes with modern monoplanes and also to build a force of bombers. There were potentially rich pickings to be had in sourcing and producing aircraft components, and the young, ambitious couple were well-placed to exploit this opportunity.

Their love-making had been tender, considerate and productive. By early 1940, John and Laura were the proud parents of a baby son and, with twins, a boy and a girl, also now on the way. Laura was always modest with her clothing. She had little time for the West End shops. So far as she was concerned, the wares of Debenhams and Marks &

Spencer were perfectly adequate to complement her strong personality and soft elegance.

The young Cresswell family would frequently seek refuge from the stresses of the business by regular weekend trips to Brighton and Hove, staying at a sensibly priced hotel. Here they would explore the joys of the town and the pier, together with stimulating family walks along the prom. However, these visits would soon be ending. Britain had declared war on Germany in the previous year, following its refusal to withdraw invading forces from Poland. The Nazi blitzkrieg had moved into Western Europe, destroying everything in its path, and German forces were now massing along the north coast of France in preparation for Operation Sea Lion, the invasion of Great Britain.

John promptly volunteered for service in the armed forces, but he had also managed to pull a few strings. He was seconded to work with the Ministry of Defence Supply, where his extensive knowledge of the intricacy of aircraft parts sourcing and manufacturing was soon found to be invaluable. He was an energetic and key member of Lord Beaverbrook's team engaged in the vital task of improving the efficiencies of aircraft manufacturing and supply. He was also involved in the "Lend/Lease" programme under which the USA provided weapons and manufacturing equipment to support Britain's war effort. John was particularly interested in acquiring American machine tools, which were far in advance of home-produced equipment. Many of these items would find their way into the growing operations of Western Engineering Limited.

The conclusion of the Second World War, in August 1945, saw a heavily indebted and war-exhausted Britain seeking to find its role in the new world. With due foresight, John had closed the car maintenance and sales part of the business in early 1940, correctly predicting that there would be minimal need and possibility for private motoring during the war. However, Western Engineering Limited had expanded hugely as a result of its wartime production of aircraft components.

John and Laura had now identified the Midlands as an area for further opportunities. Many traditional companies had staggered through the war, with Government contracts disguising their underlying inefficiencies. The truth of the situation was now becoming evident, and there were bargains to be had for those who were bold. The change of name to Midlands & West Group Limited was made in 1950 to reflect the company's widening geographic locations. An administrative and design office was set up in Birmingham, with a small Corporate Office in London's West End. A negative aspect had been the post-war Labour Government's nationalisation of certain key industries, some of which had been within the operations of the Midlands & West Group. However, John and Laura were able to use the compensation received in order to build a war chest for further growth.

They decided to use some of these funds to enable them to move their growing family to the Midlands, where most of their business operations were now located. Following an extensive search, the Bishop's Lake Estate had been identified as being the most suitable. The gated property included a large Victorian, stone-built house which was approached by a lengthy chestnut tree-lined drive. The house had eight bedrooms and a number of outbuildings, but all were in a sorry state of repair. There was a seriously neglected large fishing lake which could be brought back to life with appropriate care and then restocked. The surrounding 500 acres were let to tenant farmers, enabling the Estate to bring in a moderate income, after the deduction of management expenses and the costs of essential repairs and maintenance.

John and Laura had the necessary funds available to bring about the required transformation. In the ensuing negotiations with Bishop's Lake owners, a rapidly fading, semi-aristocratic, couple, they had agreed to relocate to a delightful, but significantly smaller, property in the locality. Now also cushioned by a substantial amount in the bank, courtesy of the Cresswell family, the former owners would be able to see out their days in appropriate style. John had not driven a rock-bottom price. He had learnt, in the world of business, that it was unproductive to seek to extract the very last penny. His rule was always to leave something on the table, because you could never be quite sure of future events.

In this case, the preservation of goodwill was an important consideration. The former owners were well-known and were still influential in the local community. John and Laura had big plans for the development of Bishop's Lake, and they would need local support to overcome possible objections. A shooting lodge was John's first priority, and then a swimming pool and spa. Laura would have preferred to reverse this order, but accepted the stronger business case for the lodge, which would facilitate the hosting of prospective customers and useful contacts. However, Laura also had her own first priority. This was for the building of stables in order to pursue her second love, which was horses. Laura's priority, of course, came first. The stables were duly constructed, and a number of well-bred hunters were acquired. John and Laura would now be spending many of their weekends at Bishop's Lake, riding out with the local hunt. Their children also grew up as competent riders, with a strong liking for horses.

John was travelling widely to inspect acquisition targets, with regular follow-up visits to ensure their effective integration into the Midlands & West Group. He now had his Pilot's Licence, together with an Instrument Rating. The next step, as had been approved by the Midlands & West Group Board of Directors, was the company's acquisition of a Miles Messenger light aircraft to be based at Coventry's Baginton Airport. During his frequent visits to the Miles Aircraft factory at Woodley, near Reading, in order to monitor the construction of the new aircraft, John could see that the factory was struggling. It had occurred to him that Miles Aircraft might be added to his list of potential acquisition targets. Annoyingly, he had been pre-empted by the aviation entrepreneur, Frederick Handley Page. However, this was probably a blessing in disguise because, twenty years later, the Handley Page business was insolvent. The unsuccessful Miles acquisition had probably played its part in bringing about this sad end.

Laura, of course, proved herself to be a highly competent and unflappable navigator. The couple flew together frequently throughout the British Isles, to the Channel Islands and to near Europe. They were often attendees at air shows and celebratory events where John was invariably recognised as being "that chap who had done something behind the scenes towards the war effort." He was never fully accepted as being an equal by the large number of post-war "Hurrah Henry" types who attended these events. They remained blissfully unaware that "that chap" had probably contributed far more to the defeat of the Nazis than most of them put together.

Chapter 3
An Unconsolable Loss

The three Cresswell children became weekly boarders at a good Midlands Independent School. John and Laura comfortably adopted the roles of Country Squire and Lady of the House at Bishop's Lake, supporting local charities and events but, at the same time, keeping a very close eye on their rapidly growing business empire. By the early 1960s, the children were finding their independence. Robert, the eldest, had recently qualified as a Solicitor, but he was not interested in being a cut-and-thrust City lawyer. He favoured Private Client work for a medium-sized legal firm in Tunbridge Wells, where it seemed he would stay. Andrew was at Art College, and his twin sister, Sandra, very much like her mother, was a community-minded and efficient person who had chosen to enter the Teaching profession. She would soon be taking up her first post in the West Country.

John and Laura now had some free time on their hands. John had taken up a liking for Havana cigars, an indulgence which Laura was happy to allow. It was at this time that John advised the Midlands & West Group Board that the company needed to acquire a London property where it could host and sometimes accommodate the growing number of overseas visiting customers and business associates. The Board agreed, and a lease was taken of a ground-floor garden apartment in London's Belgravia. Whilst the apartment was used for periodic business events, guests were never accommodated overnight. The sleeping accommodation was strictly reserved for exclusive use by members of the Cresswell family.

At the height of their amazing success, disaster was about to strike. Laura had hidden from John that she had been feeling unwell for some time. In early April 1965, she returned to the Belgravia apartment from a trip to Wimpole Street. The devastating news was that she had been diagnosed with ovarian cancer. Metastasis was already well advanced. Laura, whose fiftieth birthday the family was about to celebrate, had six months to live at the very best. John was stunned, initially unable to accept that nothing could be done. Further consultations followed, but there was no hope; only palliative care would be relevant. Despite the best care available, Laura survived less than six months. Her painful death occurred on 2 September 1965.

Approval had been obtained for the provision of two burial plots at Bishop's Lake, one for Laura and with an adjacent plot to receive her devoted husband in due course. The plots were situated on an elevated mounded area, a short walk from the house and with three hundred and sixty degree views across the Estate. In the second week of September, the Cresswell family, friends and business acquaintances gathered to say their last farewells. The chief mourner, still bereft at the loss of his Laura, wondered how he could possibly continue without her by his side. How very cruel and unfair that, in her prime of life, she had been taken from him so brutally and suddenly.

Chapter 4
Life at the Corporate Office

Laura was often in his thoughts, as she was again this Monday morning, and her framed photograph was a constant presence on his desk. The now, Sir John Cresswell, who had received his knighthood, ten years after Laura's death, for services to British Manufacturing Industry, shuddered as the memories of the awful events of 1965 returned. However, there was nothing to be gained from dwelling in the past. There was so much to be getting on with during the remainder of today. How many times had he told himself that it was unproductive to look back?

It was now just before noon. He would soon be entitled to light up his first Havana corona. One of the two cigars per day that he was allowed by Lady Eleanor. The other would be savoured in the early evening, usually with drinks, whilst he assisted Eleanor, his second wife, to entertain some of her many socialite friends at the Belgravia apartment. The very rudimentary King Street Corporate Office air conditioning system was definitely not a fan of Havana cigar smoke. However, since smoking was strictly banned elsewhere in the office, Sir John considered that a satisfactory balance had thereby been achieved; he saw no reason why he should give up another pleasure.

Sir John manoeuvred himself slowly and carefully behind his large, maroon leather-surfaced desk, trying not to enrage his already fractious back any further. He was still an impressive presence, but now at least thirty pounds above his former fighting weight. His hair was thinning and slowly greying, and he had developed jowls. His complexion was reddish and indicative of an individual with a liking for the consumption of alcohol. Sir John freely admitted to enjoying a drink, but he firmly considered himself not to be an alcoholic. Like many of the offspring of alcoholics, Sir John had a strong awareness of the perils. He could abstain from alcohol when he wished to do so, and, periodically, he did. Although he could not immediately recollect the last period of abstention. He had witnessed the consequences of going down that route, and he had determined a long time ago that he was not going to follow.

The magnificent desk was one of a number of items of antique furniture which had been deserted when the fading Midlands couple had made their escape from Bishop's Lake. Now refurbished, the desk commanded the room. The remainder of the office was furnished in modern style, including a large conference table accommodating up to ten attendees.

Since the 1950s, Sir John and Laura had been regular buyers at the Royal Academy Summer Exhibitions, and Sir John had continued to attend the event each year. As a consequence, the office walls were adorned with an eclectic variety of former exhibits. As new acquisitions were made each year, those displaced would be disposed of through the good offices of the gallery in nearby Bury Street, St James's, which was run by Sir John's younger son, Andrew.

Sir John pressed the intercom button. Miss Jennifer Palmer, in the adjacent office, anticipating his summons, answered immediately.

"Good morning, Sir John. I will bring in the diary."

Miss Palmer had reached the top of the executive secretary ladder. When at school during the Second World War years, she had been an attractive, slim and tall, teenager with strawberry blonde hair. However post-war, she had discovered, like many other women of her generation, that there was a serious deficiency of potential suitors. So many men had been lost in the war that the prospects of a good marriage were not bright. She had therefore remained a spinster and had focused on and excelled at her Pitman's shorthand courses and in developing typing skills of the highest order.

The last sixteen years had been spent at the Midlands & West Group, where Miss Palmer had employed her English Language and organisational skills in order to ensure the efficiency of the Chairman's office and the high quality of his communications. Her now greying hair was tied behind in a bun and secured with a steel pin. Her complexion had paled, and her face was lined after many years of daily commuting and office grind.

Miss Palmer was attired today in one of her usual sensible business suits, with a cream blouse beneath and adorned by a single string of pearls inherited from her recently deceased mother. Her manner could be deemed by some to be severe, but it was never foreboding. Over the years, she had sought to provide a protective cocoon around Sir John, which protection she considered to be an important part of her role.

Miss Palmer was a devoted fan of the IBM Selectric typewriter, better known as "the golf ball", and not universally popular amongst all secretaries. She considered herself to be the definitive exponent. She was certainly not interested in the sinister grey box, which she understood was something called a Personal Computer, and the associated keyboard and monitor which had recently appeared on Mike Holland's desk. The Chief Executive Officer of the Midlands & West Group, who had now been in office for just over a year, had shown worrying signs of self-sufficiency. He was hardly ever in the office, and he considered it was not necessary to have an allocated secretary.

Mike Holland's frequent absences were usually occasioned by the need to troubleshoot across what had now become the somewhat disparate Midlands & West Group. On the rare occasions that Mike Holland was in the office, he appeared able to communicate with his team through the use of the said grey box and utilising the concept of something called email. Miss Palmer had no intention of getting involved in such horrors and, fortunately, Sir John appeared to be similarly disinclined.

Miss Palmer's reward for her dedication had been a small flat in Barking, with the mortgage now almost paid off, and a daily train journey into Liverpool Street Station. Then an uncomfortable trip on the Underground to Piccadilly, a stimulating walk along Jermyn Street and a left turn into St James's Square. Only just two years to go now until the receipt of her pension from the M&W Group Final Salary Pension Scheme. Other small pensions and modest savings would then enable her future life to revolve around the Lawn Bowls Club, together with the weekly lunches with kindred souls from the local Historical Society and the Book Club. There would also be attendance at the monthly meetings of the Rotary Club's Inner Wheel, where she had served as an officer for many years. She would also continue her annual visits to the Isle of Wight, staying with an elderly aunt, her mother's younger sister, with whom she regularly corresponded.

Hopefully, she would have no issues in reaching the milestone of retirement, unlike her fellow spinster and former executive secretary colleague, Edith, her workplace friend, lunching companion and confidant. For many years, Edith had loyally supported the unimaginative and overly compliant Midlands & West Group Finance Director in his continuing and progressively more difficult attempts to balance the Books. When equilibrium was eventually reached, it was often achieved only by promptly closing down those offending businesses which had failed, even if only marginally, to meet their prescribed business plan targets.

Whilst Edith had received no formal financial training, she was experienced and astute enough to recognise the growing danger signals. However, there appeared to be no such recognition amongst the bright young things in the Finance Department. They seemed content to carry on in wilful ignorance of potential disasters ahead. Edith had concluded that such a situation could not continue indefinitely.

Just under twelve months ago, Edith had suddenly gone missing without explanation. A week later, she had returned to the office

16

adorned with bandages and a sling, reluctantly admitting to having undergone unspecified local surgery. Eight months later, there had been another absence, but this time there would be no return to the office. Poor Edith had been taken by the nodular melanoma, which had aggressively ravaged through her system.

Her replacement in the Finance Director's office was one of the said bright young things. The promising twenty-five-year-old in question now rejoiced under the title of "Personal Assistant." Other than her efficient telephone manner, her abilities appeared, to Miss Palmer, not to extend much beyond the transcription of audio tapes. Miss Palmer, or "Miss Perfect", as she was sometimes referred to by the said bright young things, when out of earshot, preferred not to contemplate the standard of literacy of the letters which were now emerging from the Finance Department.

"Will you be lunching out today, Sir John?"

"Yes, I'm meeting Andrew at the Garrick at 12.30," he replied. "Please ask Gerry to bring up the car from the basement in ten minutes' time. Now, is there anything else?"

"Sir Adrian McClean will be here at 3.00 pm; he has been requesting the meeting for some time."

This could be an interesting meeting, thought Sir John. Sir Adrian was the Founder and Chairman of Britain's so-called Second Force Independent Airline, Anglo-Scottish Airways. Sir John knew the company was not having the best of times; he wondered what the celebrated Scottish aviator had in mind.

"Thank you, Miss Palmer, please contact Mr Lawrence Marshfield at British International and ask him to be over here at 2.30 for a pre-meeting about Anglo-Scottish. Now, please tell Mr Shining to report to me immediately."

Chapter 5
Jennifer and Harry

Jennifer Palmer returned to her large adjacent office, which included a visitors' waiting area. Here she was able to exercise her cocooning duties by mounting guard over the access to Sir John's office. Unbeknown to new visitors, there was also a carefully hidden second door to the Chairman's office through which it was possible to exit direct into the main office corridor. When necessary, this door could be used to dispose of time-expired visitors into the main office, without them being sighted by in-comers assembled in the waiting area. For Sir John, the maintenance of separation and of strict secrecy was considered essential. The second door also provided a convenient escape route for the Chairman, should he need to make a quick exit.

She picked up the internal phone. "Harry, he wants to see you now, and he is not in a good mood."

Harold Edward Shining had anticipated the call. Mondays would not be the same without his usual session with the Chairman and the low-level confrontations that then often ensued. It was part of the price he had had to pay for his rescue three years ago.

Harry braced himself to his full medium height in preparation for the forthcoming drama. Moustachioed, lean, and still quite fit, Harry was dressed today in his usual Marks & Spencer slacks and sports jacket. He had something of a military manner about him, having joined the RAF just before the end of the Second World War, and he had then stayed in the Service working primarily on radar installations.

Harry considered himself to be a creative person, and on completing his service with the RAF, he joined a Midlands & West Group subsidiary, based in Kingston, specialising in office equipment and systems. This role had given some vent to what Harry believed were his hitherto unrecognised creative talents. There had been some successes, but a disastrous investment in a Harry Shining-invented rotary binding system, designed to provide flexibility and efficiency, had proved, in operation, to do precisely the opposite. The installed systems had needed to be removed, and the competition had rapidly moved in with superior technology. The Midlands & West Group accountants had then descended, with the inevitable consequences.

Sir John had personally reviewed the redundancy list and had determined that, provided he kept his creative inclinations under control, Harry was a suitable person to take on the role of Office Manager at King Street. Following his normal practice, Sir John had fixed the annual salary at five per cent over the going rate. The rationale being his belief that, if you slightly overpaid people, then they would be more inclined to go the extra mile; they might even show some loyalty!

Harry was not greatly enthusiastic about the prospect of a daily commute into Central London. However, he had decided, at the time, that the preservation of his pension from the M&W Group Final Salary Pension Scheme had to be the priority. There were then only five years to go before he clocked up the thirty years' service with the Group, which would mean a pension of around half of his current and now slightly enhanced salary. He had therefore accepted the Corporate Office job, also deciding that, since commuting was inevitable, he might as well commute from the location which he had selected for his retirement.

Accordingly, a house move had been made to a small bungalow which had been identified in Hove, quite close to where Harry's daughter and son-in-law lived with their two children. The couple ran a local estate agency, and Harry envisaged that, post-retirement, they would doubtless be grateful for his availability to provide general assistance in the business. For example, he could show properties to applicants. However, he had not yet got around to consulting the couple about this matter.

"Just look at it!"

"Good afternoon, Sir John, just look at what?"

Sir John peered at Harry over his steel-rimmed, half-moon spectacles. His piercing blue eyes, which had so often chilled both business rivals and inept profession advisers alike, were still giving excellent long sight, but he had conceded the need for assistance for reading purposes.

"There, of course, on the desk." Sir John was pointing to the collection of ornate Waterford Glass ink-wells, placed on a large silver plate. Together with their associated silver-coated writing implements, they occupied the centre of the maroon leather. Most of these items had been discovered when John and Laura had explored the further reaches of Bishop's Lake, after gaining possession back in 1950.

"How many times have I told you that I expect to start the week with everything clean and in order. There are ink smears and dust everywhere. Surely a bit of attention is not too much to ask for."

"I do apologise, Sir John, but it has been a very busy morning. There was a bit of a crisis with the office toilets, and I have been arranging for plumbers and then for a thorough clean-up. Also, I had to negotiate with the Third Floor for the temporary use of their loos."

"What nonsense, I visited the Gents only ten minutes after arriving this morning and everything was perfectly in order."

"Yes, Sir John, you are of course referring to the executive conveniences, to which only you and your direct reports have access."

"Please don't argue with me, Mr Shining, just make sure that everything is tickety boo by the time I get back from lunch. Now I must go, Gerry is waiting with the car for me downstairs."

"Oh, and by the way, the cook has been complaining to Lady Eleanor that the oven in the office kitchen needs cleaning."

Harry was fighting a constant and losing battle with the said prima-donna cook, who was hired in from time to time when it was decided to host a client lunch or a dinner at the Corporate Office. She was an excellent cook, but her hygiene standards were definitely questionable. She also considered it was beneath her to clean up the kitchen messes that she had created.

Harry decided to chance his arm. "Sir John, the only person who uses the oven is the cook. We work here on the principle that the oven and the kitchen area generally should be left in the same state of cleanliness in which they are found."

"Please don't argue with me again, Mr Shining, just fix it. Now I must go."

Sir John decided to exit through the escape door, rather than to brave any further interrogation by Miss Palmer. He considered these clashes with Harry to be relatively harmless. With his long-discovered powers of empathy, he was aware of Harry's popularity around the office. Harry was willing, if not always able, to tackle the practical issues, and he was a sympathetic listener and support when the younger staff had problems. There was nothing to be gained in generating bad will. In any event, finding a suitable replacement for Harry would be difficult.

Harry returned to his work station in the main office and instructed specialist cleaning contractors to attend to the kitchen later that day. He collected together suitable cleaning materials for the tasks required at the maroon leather desk. Everything would be to Sir John's satisfaction by the time he was back from lunch.

One certain thing was that Harry would be leaving King Street at his usual 16.01 hours, and then heading briskly for Victoria Station in order to catch the Brighton train. He and his wife would later be able to take their customary early evening walk along the seafront at Hove and to enjoy the sunset, possibly in company with some of their grandchildren.

Chapter 6
A Disturbing Appointment

Miss Palmer gracefully navigated her way through her lunchtime sandwich. Monday was prawn salad on brown bread, accompanied by freshly-squeezed orange juice and followed by an apple. One luxury, which she allowed herself, was for her sandwiches to be prepared by the local Italian-owned sandwich shop. Here she was a regular and much valued customer, purchasing not only for herself but for the frequent working lunches held at the Corporate Office. The shop would happily deliver, although in the summer months, Miss Palmer would usually collect her sandwiches in person. She would then enjoy them mid-way during her regular walks in nearby St James's Park or in Green Park. From now on, these lunchtime walks would be considerably less convivial without the company of her dear friend Edith.

The whole of this British International Airlines business and Sir John's appointment as its Chairman, she ruminated, had been most inconvenient and disturbing. She considered it was also totally unnecessary. Instead of a gentle run-down to retirement, she had now found that the meeting frequency at King Street had more than doubled. This situation was entirely due to the affairs of British International. Sir John also had a Chairman's office at the British International Hounslow Headquarters, so why didn't its meetings take place there? The answer was probably that Sir John disliked the trip out to the west of London, and so he usually only went to Hounslow once a month. Perhaps the journey reminded him of his humble start in life as a trainee mechanic, but those days were now more than fifty years distant!

Sir John and Lady Eleanor already had a wonderful life with absolutely no financial concerns. The Midlands & West Group effectively funded their London living arrangements, and then there was the seemingly endless round of social events. The summer programme was just about to commence, first with the Chelsea Flower Show and then concluding with opera at the Glyndebourne Festival in the autumn. Corporate hospitality would flow generously at each event. The superb house and Estate at Bishop's Lake provided every possible weekend comfort with its beautiful furnishings and the spa and swimming pool. Also, the stable of fabulous horses and the now fully-operational and well-stocked fishing lake, not to mention the shooting lodge. A resident staff was present to service the occupants' every need.

The Conservative Government had been in power since 1979, and Sir John was feted as being one of its favourite business people. However, it had taken the Government more than five years to approach Sir John, requesting him to rescue its failing State-owned airline, then known as British Empire Airways. Sir John considered that those critical five years had been wasted. He had driven quite a hard bargain with the Government, including obtaining agreement that the Airline would take an assignment of the remaining term of the Belgravia apartment lease from the Midlands & West Group. It would replace the Rolls-Royce Silver Spirit, when it was due for change, and the Airline would also make a handsome contribution to the Midlands & West Group for its access to and use of the Group's King Street offices.

As it was currently Government-owned, there was a constraint on the level of fees payable for the Chairmanship of British Empire Airways. However, Sir John envisaged that this amount would be reviewed substantially upwards, as and when a successful flotation was achieved and the Airline became a public company. He would also receive a substantial share allocation upon flotation, with subsequent allotments in the following years. Overall, the compensation flowing in future years from this appointment should be sufficiently rewarding.

Sir John's initial five years term of office had been effective from 1 June 1985. After many years of working with him, Miss Palmer, of course, knew exactly why he had taken on the role as Airline Chairman. Power and influence were a part of the answer, together with Sir John's obsession with "The British Establishment", whatever that might mean, and of being accepted as a member thereof. He wished to distance himself from the "mechanic made good" tag and, despite his many successes, he still appeared to believe on occasions that "the other man's grass is always greener". Consequently, he continued to drive himself forward, constantly striving to ascend ever higher in Society and to prove himself to be better and the best.

British Empire Airways had commenced post-war operations on 1 January 1946 as the successor to the pre-Second World War Imperial Airways. The "Imperial" days were clearly over, and, around the Nation, all references to "Imperial" were being quietly dropped. However, those in charge at the time seemed to believe, by their decision to include "Empire" in the name of the new State-owned corporation, that nothing had or would change significantly. There was an apparent assumption that Britain's Empire would continue indefinitely, but the reality was very different. There was unrest in many parts of the Empire, and independence would be granted progressively to the vast majority of its constituents over the next thirty years.

The first and eminently sensible action of Sir John, following his appointment, had been to change the Airline's name by replacing "Empire" with "International" and "Airways" with "Airlines". Sir John's second action had been to slim down the British International Airlines Board from the then fifteen incumbents. This process had involved the controversial removal of a number of retired ex-senior RAF officers, former airline executive directors, and all political appointees. The new Board of ten members would comprise individuals who were well-known to Sir John, and they were selected for their track records in Catering, Finance, Logistics, Information Technology, and Marketing & Sales. Only two existing incumbents would be retained for their expertise in Aircraft Selection and Maintenance and in Flight Operations and Safety.

Sir John's third action had been to start the process for the appointment of a new Chief Executive Officer. For this purpose, he had looked across St James's Square to where the offices of a leading International "Head Hunter" were located. The firm had been duly instructed, and the net had been cast widely. Lawrence Marshfield had eventually been put forward as the best match and the most suitable candidate.

Sir John had carried out the final interview personally, and he had applied the normal two evaluation tests which he always used when making appointments. First, did the candidate have the required skills and experience, and second, did he like the individual? Lawrence Marshfield had passed both tests. He certainly had appropriate skills and an impressive track record. Sir John had taken a warming towards this apparently modest and self-effacing person, who he also thought might possibly be susceptible to some gentle manipulation. Marshfield was also unlikely to pose a threat to Sir John's Chairmanship and, particularly, to challenge his intention to secure a second term of office from June 1990. The Board proceeded to accept Sir John's recommendation for the appointment of Lawrence Marshfield as the Chief Executive Officer of British International Airlines, to be effective from 1 January 1986.

Chapter 7
The Young Lawrence

Lawrence Marshfield was the youngest of three sons of Edward "Ted" Marshfield and his wife, Betty. Ted Marshfield had served with distinction as a Navigation Officer in the Merchant Navy during the Second World War. He had remained in the Service after the cessation of hostilities, but he had soon been invalided out. He had been struck by a broken hawser when on deck supervising an unloading exercise. The hawser had occasioned internal organ damage from which Ted had made a partial recovery, but insufficient to enable him to continue his much-loved career at sea.

Some financial compensation was received, including a modest disablement pension, which, together with their accumulated savings, had facilitated the purchase by Lawrence's parents of a sub-post office in Tranmere on the Wirral, including a tobacconist and sweets shop. There was a good-sized living accommodation on the first and second floors. The Marshfield family settled into their new life, and Ted hated every minute of it. He would frequently relieve the monotony for short periods by taking the ferry across the Mersey to the Liverpool main docks in order to look enviously at the latest cargo ships and liners. He would return regretful at the loss of his previous career at sea, but renewed with just about sufficient motivation to continue the daily slog of being a sub-postmaster and shopkeeper in Tranmere.

Lawrence's two older brothers were outgoing types who enjoyed their football far more than their academic studies. Neither had distinguished themselves in the Eleven Plus examination, which at that time effectively determined secondary educational futures. Both boys had been content to attend the local Secondary Modern School, to which Eleven Plus failures were consigned. They played football for the school and later were equally content to take up local Engineering apprenticeships, well-suited to their excellent practical skills. Afterwards, they would be able to obtain regular and relatively secure employment in the area, to continue playing amateur football, and to accompany their father to the home matches of Tranmere Rovers FC.

From an appearance point of view, everything about Lawrence was pretty average. Average height and average looks, straight hair and brown eyes. He was an introverted boy who was not remotely interested in football. He was much more concerned with the functioning of the sub-post office and with the operations of the associated tobacconist and sweets business. On Saturday afternoons, he would sit down with Betty, as she wrote up the accounts and carried out stock-takes. His mother soon became aware of her youngest son's ability with numbers and of his rapid grasp of the principles of running a business.

When the time for the Eleven Plus arrived, Lawrence was placed in the top ten percent of passes in the Local Educational Authority area, including achieving the maximum possible marks in Arithmetic. As a result, in September 1954, Lawrence started his secondary education at the local Grammar School. Here he continued to excel in Mathematics and in Science subjects, whilst performing adequately in Arts subjects.

In common with most Grammar Schools at the time, Rugby Union was the designated winter sport at Lawrence's school. Rugby Union was not an ideal sport for a boy of slight build and with an academic nature. However, Lawrence was not to be deterred, and he soon found that the position of full back suited his limited abilities. He became established as the Second XV full back, where he was certainly not a threat to Geoff Prescott in the First XV. Geoff was an excellent athlete and a far stronger attacking player than Lawrence. Geoff and Lawrence would often train together, and Geoff soon came to have a good regard for the junior player. He appeared to have outstanding spatial awareness, an ability that enabled him to predict with uncanny accuracy almost exactly where the ball would land and how the game would flow. He also admired Lawrence's courage and tenacity. Lawrence was usually the last line of defence and, whilst the Second XV lost more matches than it won, the score differences would have been much greater without Lawrence's heroic efforts in the back line.

Academic success continued with excellent results in the General Certificate of Education, which Lawrence took early at the age of fifteen. He then progressed to the Sixth Form, studying Mathematics and Science subjects at "A level", and completed his secondary education in the summer of 1961 with three Grade A passes. An extremely notable achievement at the time. Although Lawrence was clearly the first person in his family who appeared destined to attend University, he had then stunned his parents with the startling news that he was going to sea in the autumn.

During the summer, Lawrence had visited the Liverpool Offices of Oceanic Transport & Trading Limited (OTT) and had been successfully interviewed for the position of Trainee Purser. He would now be commencing a career at sea, in mid-autumn, aboard one of the majestic ocean liners operated by OTT. The majority of passengers who wished to cross the North Atlantic were still travelling by sea. Betty was obviously much saddened that she would now be seeing her youngest son much less frequently, not to mention the loss of his much-valued services in the business. Ted was quietly pleased, although he did not express any opinion. He would, of course, have preferred Lawrence to have signed on as a Navigation Officer, for which role he clearly had the required abilities. However, at least the family connection with the sea was to be resumed.

Chapter 8
Lawrence and Lisa

Lawrence soon gained his sea legs and much enjoyed his first job with OTT. His outstanding abilities were quickly recognised and, within three years, he was a fully qualified Purser and also studying to become an American-qualified Certified Public Accountant. He had determined that his future career prospects would most probably lie in America. In 1965, OTT decided that Lawrence's talents were being wasted by remaining at sea, and so he was offered a mid-level finance role in the New York office. Five years later, at the tender age of twenty-seven, Lawrence Marshfield was appointed Chief Financial Officer of the OTT American business.

Lawrence had become aware that there were three levels of competence in Finance. First, there was the correct identification and recording of figures, the bookkeeping stage. Then there was the assembling and ordering of figures and ensuring their compliance with the required Accounting Standards, the Accounts production stage. The third level was the interpretation and presentation of the figures. Many Accountants were good at the first two stages but weak at the third stage. Lawrence excelled at level three. His spatial reasoning abilities enabled him to take a "helicopter view," and he had discovered an outstanding ability to present figures to senior colleagues in an understandable manner and with clarity as to their implications and the future actions required.

Lawrence had also learned one other important lesson from an old hand who had mentored him during his traineeship. This lesson was simple: "Never distort or hide embarrassing figures, because bad news only gets worse". Lawrence had resolved that he would always report the correct figures and that he would tell the truth, however painful that might be.

It would be a further five years before Lawrence's next promotion, but it was to be a significant move. In 1975, at the startlingly young age of thirty-two, Lawrence Marshfield was appointed as Chief Executive Officer of the OTT American business, also with a place on the main OTT Executive Board. He would now be making regular trips to the UK, usually flying over, as was the growing preference for most passengers, but returning from meetings on OTT's liners whenever his schedule allowed. With the rapidly growing availability of Personal Computers, the time spent on board could be used productively.

Lisa Spencer was born in Staines in 1955, and she had excelled as a gymnast and dancer. She had also joined a local Theatre Group, which had connections with Theatrical Agencies providing dancers and actors to hotels and to cruise operators. Lisa had obtained her first dance contract with OTT in 1976. She had since become a firm favourite, and within a year, she was a Dance Captain.

Whenever he was on board an OTT liner, it was Lawrence's practice to provide a short business update to the Captain and his team. It was when attending one of these briefings that Lisa had first seen this average-looking and modest, but clearly fiercely intelligent and determined individual. Although twelve years her senior, she did not see the age difference as an issue. There was a strange and compelling attraction.

Lawrence had also become aware of this fabulously attractive, naturally blonde-haired young woman. Eventually, he plucked up the courage to invite Lisa to join him for drinks in the Owner's Suite. Lisa's curt response to what Lawrence had innocently regarded as being his innocuous invitation had been:

"Are you aware, Mr Marshfield, that there is a very active grapevine on this ship? And, anyway, what kind of a girl do you take me for?"

Lawrence, suitably admonished, was in the process of rapidly creeping back into his shell when he was highly relieved to hear Lisa's parting comment:

"I might be prepared to consider an invitation to dinner when we reach New York, provided, of course, that your doubtless extremely busy schedule will allow."

No matter how busy his schedule was, Lawrence made sure that it allowed for whatever date Lisa specified for dinner. An occasion was duly determined, and a meal was much enjoyed at a top New York restaurant. Lisa had then informed Lawrence that, in accordance with her contract, she was returning to the ship and did so promptly. Thereafter, Lawrence became a frequent visitor to the OTT liner schedules, checking on Lisa's whereabouts and ensuring that he was available for further "occasions" whenever she was in port.

Many dinners and attendances at Broadway shows had followed, and the relationship had continued to grow and strengthen. Lawrence was clearly besotted, and Lisa had begun to appreciate that this conscientious and very able man was a cut above most of the types she had met since she had been at sea. This was most certainly not a case of a junior employee being attracted to the boss for his money or position. Lisa knew that she was of much more value to OTT than the company was to her. Also, she was not short of offers for work and marriage; she had already turned down many suitors to date, and there would doubtless be lots more.

The relationship was eventually consummated. For Lawrence, after such a long and respectful wait, the opportunity to take the relationship to the next level and to explore the mysteries of Lisa's warm, curvaceous, and well-toned body was a great joy. Lisa considered Lawrence to be a competent and considerate lover, in contrast to most of her relatively few previous relationships. Lawrence had subsequently proposed to Lisa. She had accepted, and the knot was to be tied at the New York, Manhattan City Hall over Easter 1980.

Geoff Prescott, who, after a very successful playing career, was now the coach of a leading Premiership Rugby Union Club, had readily accepted Lawrence's invitation to be Best Man. He had insisted that he and his wife would fly over to New York at their own expense. Lawrence had equally insisted that, after the wedding and celebrations, they would travel back home at his expense in the Owner's Suite aboard OTT's latest transatlantic liner.

At the ceremony, Lisa looked magnificent in her couture wedding gown and was supported by five of her dance group colleagues in stunning matching outfits. The Wedding Reception was held at the Waldorf Astoria Hotel, with both sets of parents being present and thoroughly enjoying the successes of their respective offspring. It was also an opportunity for them to experience their first taste of America, which, at that time, was a very different place from both Staines and Tranmere.

All members of the OTT New York office had been invited to the Reception and all had attended. It was not a matter of obligation or of seeking to ingratiate themselves with the boss. Everyone present was there out of a genuine desire to wish this much-admired and well-liked couple every happiness and joy in their years ahead together.

In accepting Lawrence's proposal, Lisa had made just two stipulations. First, that she would continue working until she decided to retire, and second, that, if there were children, the family would relocate to the UK, where they would be brought up and educated. As matters evolved, Lisa did not continue working for long. Their first child was born in the following year, and a second two years later. Lawrence had already decided that it was time to make a career move away from OTT and had put himself in the shop window. The invitation to join British International Airlines as Chief Executive Officer had followed.

Lawrence, Lisa and their children had completed their move to the UK in December 1985. They had settled comfortably into a mid-sized property in the exclusive St George's Hill Estate at Weybridge, close to Lisa's parents and within easy striking distance of the British International Headquarters at Hounslow and the two London airports. The couple and their young family now looked forward to the next phase of their lives. Lisa fully intended to be a hands-on Mum, but there should still be time for her to help out with dance training and choreography at the local gymnastics club, one of the most successful in the Country.

Chapter 9
A Troubled Competitor

Miss Palmer welcomed her first visitor of the day. He was not at all visually impressive, but the recently joined British International Chief Executive Officer, Lawrence Marshfield, had at least arrived early for his Monday afternoon meeting with Sir John. Also, he had previously called Miss Palmer to enquire if permission could be granted for him to use the horrible machine on Mike Holland's desk. She had checked with Mike Holland, who was fully in agreement and pleased that at least one other Chief Executive was computer literate. The modest individual was now engrossed in the workings of the nasty grey box, and Lawrence Marshfield had started to scribble down what was, presumably, some of the information emitting from the unpleasant device.

Sir John had quietly re-accessed his office through the escape door. Lunch at the Garrick had been enjoyable, although his Club preference was for Whites, which was a short walk away from the Corporate Office in nearby St James's Street. Whites was where he had built up a wide network of influential contacts. He had joined the Garrick more recently, primarily to infiltrate the Arts world and thereby possibly to provide some assistance to the fortunes of Andrew's Art Gallery. In that regard, mid-way through lunch, Andrew had mentioned that a few sales had fallen through during the month and, consequently, he was a little strapped for cash. In particular, payment of the Gallery rental was imminent.

Hardly a surprise to Sir John, in fact, this situation was a rather regular occurrence. As usual, Sir John had agreed to provide appropriate funding with promises from Andrew that the amount would be repaid as soon as sales improved. Previous "loans," of course, seemed to have been quietly forgotten, and Sir John did not expect there to be any variation on this occasion. On the positive side, at least he saw Andrew on a regular basis. These meetings were in contrast to his infrequent contact with his other two children. He often had the uncomfortable feeling that they were seeking to avoid a close association.

Despite his financial woes, Andrew was a good boy who appeared to be happy in life, living with his companion, George, at their modest flat in Bermondsey. George was a very successful make-up artist, working in Television, whom Andrew had met at Art College. Although George's skills were of no particular interest or use to Sir John, he was impressed by people who had talent and who were good at their jobs. George had therefore passed evaluation test number one. Sir John had also formed an instant liking for him and so the second test was also satisfied. At a time when the HIV/Aids epidemic was raging across the world, Sir John's primary concern was simply that the relationship would be secure and would remain monogamous.

"Has Mr Marshfield arrived?"

"Yes, Sir John," Miss Palmer responded, "He is working on that awful machine in Mike Holland's office. I will ask him to join you immediately."

Miss Palmer entered Mike Holland's office, and Lawrence hurriedly closed down the Personal Computer.

"Sir John is now ready for you, Mr Marshfield. I see you have some papers there on the table. May I be of any assistance to you?"

"Well, actually, Miss Palmer, I have just drafted this letter," said Lawrence, holding up the crumpled piece of paper which contained the recent outpourings of the grey box.

"We have a new arrangement at Hounslow where we have just two secretaries, although we call them personal assistants nowadays, to service the top Executive team. The arrangement is on a last-come, last-served basis. It works fine, but because I am so often in meetings, I usually find myself at the back of the queue."

"Please let me have it, Mr Marshfield. Is there anything else?"

Lawrence scrambled in his briefcase and produced several other rough drafts of letters, which looked as though their contents had also previously emerged from a grey box.

Miss Palmer took all of them from Lawrence, commenting, "These letters will be ready for you to sign when your meeting with Sir John is over."

Lawrence entered Sir John's office. Sir John pointed to the conference table, and the Chairman sat down, together with his new Chief Executive Officer, with whom he was already considerably impressed.

"Well, how are things going? It's amazing how time flies. I think you have been with us, Lawrence, for over four months now. I thought it would be useful to have an update on Anglo-Scottish, because I have a meeting shortly with Sir Adrian McClean, its Chairman. He is a canny old devil, and I need to know where he might be coming from."

"Good afternoon, Chairman," said Lawrence. "I am settling in well and everything is progressing pretty satisfactorily, but there is clearly much still to be done at British International if we are to achieve the Government's target to float the company on The Stock Exchange within three years of your appointment. I understand that is the Prime Minister's target."

"Correct, the flotation target date is the end of May 1988," answered Sir John.

"So we have just about two years from now," said Lawrence.

"I suggest we aim to present a detailed flotation plan to the Department of Trade and Industry at the beginning of 1988. There will still be some final key issues at that point, which only discussions with the Department will be capable of resolving."

"Yes, I agree," said Sir John. "There are a number of barriers to be surmounted, but I have every confidence in you, Lawrence. The new Board is very knowledgeable, and it seems to me that you are making progress in building a capable Executive team around you. Now what about the Anglo-Scottish situation?"

Lawrence reached into his briefcase again, this time for some worksheets which he had previously prepared on his Personal Computer at Hounslow. "Do you mind if I show you a few figures?"

"If you must," responded Sir John, "I see you are still using that funny machine of yours. Is it of any real use, or is it just a gimmick to impress?"

"Definitely not a gimmick, Chairman. I predict that, within five years, every Senior Executive will be using a Personal Computer, possibly even yourself."

"I very much doubt that, but please continue."

Lawrence opened the worksheets, which showed the Anglo-Scottish profit and loss figures for the past five years, together with the latest estimate for the current year's performance. It was very evident that the airline was having a difficult time in 1986. It had become seriously loss-making and the prospects for future years were looking bleak.

"Very interesting. Are these figures correct, and why the sudden deterioration in performance?"

Lawrence responded;

"The earlier years' figures are definitely correct, because they are taken from published information. The current year's figures are based on what we know from our own operations. Many Americans are not travelling long-haul because of the terrorist threat currently posed by Libya. Also, the possible implications of the reactor meltdown last month at the Russian Chernobyl Nuclear Power Plant have occasioned a big drop in optional long-haul travel for leisure purposes. Further, we believe that Business Class bookings for Anglo-Scottish have been particularly affected by the Nigerian currency devaluation, together with fewer oil company executives travelling Business Class due to the drop in the oil price. Altogether, it is not a pretty sight."

Most interesting thought, Sir John. Perhaps Sir Adrian has decided that it is time for him to make a quiet exit. Anglo-Scottish had most definitely become surplus to requirements nowadays. Sir John recollected that there had been a previous British Empire Airways attempt to restrict the operations of Scott-Air, which was the predecessor of Anglo-Scottish. Maybe the time had now arrived to do the job properly?

Miss Palmer buzzed through on the intercom. "Sir Adrian McClean has arrived, Sir John."

"Fine, please tell him that I will be available in just a few minutes."

"Before you go, Lawrence, could you just run through, very briefly, those key flotation issues to which you referred earlier?"

"In summary, Chairman, they are aircraft fleet replacement and rationalisation, employment reduction by at least fifteen thousand heads, increasing market share generally, and also achieving significantly reduced pensions costs and liabilities. The overall aim is to lower our cost base, to eliminate unprofitable operations, and to increase our competitive position in all of the markets that we serve."

"Well, that all seems very sensible and appropriate. There is clearly plenty to be getting on with. Just before you go, what do you think of this?"

Sir John pushed across the table the latest issue of "Aviation News". The headline was "Atlantic Fortress doubles capacity."

"I am aware of this development, Chairman and it is factually correct."

"Factually correct, my foot. Just the mere use of that Fortress name alone really grates on me. So far as I am concerned, it is completely and deliberately misleading. It implies size and strength, but, as we are perfectly well aware, all that "Laughing Boy" has done is simply to lease another clapped-out Jumbo. He now has two of them, big deal! I understand these aircraft are operated by geriatric flight crews, with dolly birds on board attempting to provide a glitzy in-flight service. I also object to the garish orange livery of their aircraft and particularly to the stylised "F" on the tail and nose. It seems to me that he is just cocking a snoot at us."

"I hear what you say, Chairman, but I think you are being a little unfair. Atlantic Fortress is a credible operation, but it is small and only has permission to operate from Gatwick. So it is not currently a significant threat to us."

"So you say, but I suggest you keep a close eye on the situation."

"Laughing Boy" was Sir John's nickname for Tommy Branscombe, the entrepreneur who had founded Atlantic Fortress Airways two years previously, in early 1984. Lawrence had decided that now was not the time to acquaint Sir John with a piece of relevant information which would enrage him further. The geriatric flight crews, he had mentioned, were mostly comprised of ex-British International personnel. They had been recruited by Branscombe from amongst a pool of pilots and flight engineers who had taken advantage of the generous early retirement packages currently on offer from British International!

Sir John rose awkwardly from the conference table and directed Lawrence towards the escape door; he did not want to run the risk of Sir Adrian intercepting Lawrence in Miss Palmer's adjacent office. Lawrence was pleased that the meeting was over. He waited momentarily in the main office corridor before re-entering Miss Palmer's office after Sir Adrian had exited.

"Oh, there you are. Here are your letters, Mr Marshfield."

Miss Palmer handed over four letters, immaculately typed on British International letterhead. The contents of the letters, as drafted by Lawrence, had been very precise and methodically ordered, but, in Miss Palmer's view, they were much lacking in elegance and flair. Consequently, she had made a few subtle changes and improvements. Lawrence quickly read the letters, privately noted the changes, and started to put the letters into his briefcase.

"Is everything in order, Mr Marshfield?"

"Very much so", replied Lawrence.

"Well, in that case, please sign the letters and I will ensure they are posted first class."

"Are you quite sure?"

"Yes, I am entirely sure, so please be on your way."

Chapter 10
The Jovial Scotsman

Miss Palmer's second visitor of the afternoon had been a very different personality. Not at all the dour Scot she had been expecting, but a quite relaxed, outgoing, and jovial individual. Physically small and well-rounded in stature, but with a big personality, Sir Adrian had immediately engaged Miss Palmer in conversation. He had rapidly found out about Miss Palmer's Lawn Bowling skills and, being a bit of a bowler himself, they had discovered common ground.

Apart from the fact that the two airline Chairmen had both become Knights of the Realm at the same investiture ceremony in 1975, they had little else in common, other than their humble origins and their mutual likes of Havana cigars. McClean, the son of a Glasgow railwayman, was a young boy in the Second World War who had become fascinated with aeroplanes during the Battle of Britain. He had later passed the aptitude tests and had joined the RAF at age seventeen. By the age of twenty-one, he was playing scrum half for the RAF's Rugby Union team. He was also co-piloting the RAF's lumbering and geriatric, four-engine transport planes as they delivered and collected troops around the world from Britain's steadily declining Empire involvements.

After completing twelve years of RAF service, Adrian McClean had then joined a small Independent British airline operating charter passenger and freight services and using the civil equivalents of the obsolete transports operated by the RAF. McClean's former Squadron Adjutant was working for the same airline in flight operations and aircraft maintenance. The two ex-RAF officers had then got together and decided that they could do better. A small group of investors led by

McClean and his colleague, and including the Overseas Travel Association as a major investor, then formed the UK's newest independent airline, Scott-Air. With a start-up fund of nearly half a million pounds, the new airline had then approached British Empire Airways for the provision of one of its redundant Douglas DC-7Cs.

A fleet of ten of these aircraft, the last of the highly successful American Douglas piston engine types, which had been the backbone of long-haul travel during the 1950s, had been acquired by British Empire Airways as an emergency purchase, made necessary because of extensive delays in the development of the turboprop Bristol Britannia. By the time that the Britannias eventually arrived, they had been largely superseded by the formidable pure jet, American-built, Boeing 707s and Douglas DC-8s, both of which offered higher cruising speeds, passenger capacities, and superior economics.

The Flight Operations team at British Empire had a big problem with two effectively redundant types on their hands, and so the approach by Scott-Air was much welcomed. It was agreed that a DC-7C would be provided under an ACMI (Aircraft, Crew, Maintenance, and Insurance) contract. British Empire Airways would supply crews (although McClean and some of the other investors would also pilot) and it would service and insure the aircraft. The Flight Operations team was relieved to have at least one aircraft off its hands and generating revenue, whilst longer-term disposal options for the two obsolete fleets were explored. It did not seem to occur to British Empire Airways' higher management that they were effectively setting up a potential future competitor.

The first Scott-Air service took place in early 1962, and the new airline was soon running regular charter flights, mainly to Africa. All was going well until disaster struck three months later when the DC-7C crashed on take-off from Mozambique, killing all on board. This was a terrible tragedy, but a subsequent investigation absolved Scott-Air of fault. However, a number of investors had taken fright, and

McClean had been required to use all of his courage and resolve to buy them out in order to ensure that Scott-Air would survive.

The aircraft had been fully insured against all contingencies, and British Empire Airways was very willing and able to provide a replacement. There had been no subsequent disasters and, in the following years, Scott-Air had progressively increased its fleet and operations, primarily using ex-British Empire DC-7Cs and also some of its Britannias now displaced from mainstream services.

Sir Adrian, out of his natural enthusiasm and due to an element of naivety, had then made an error. Scott-Air had established weekly services from the UK to the Bahamas and to Bermuda and was considering offering onward flights to the East Coast of America. This activity had been identified by British Empire Airways as being a serious potential threat to its transatlantic services. In late 1965, British Empire Airways had approached Sir Adrian with a proposal to take a fifty-one percent holding in Scott-Air.

Although this deal and tie-up with British Empire Airways would mean his loss of control of Scott-Air, Sir Adrian would retain a senior management role and would also have a place on the British Empire Airways Board. He genuinely believed that the two airlines would be able to work well in partnership and to develop worldwide air services for the benefit of the United Kingdom.

Sir Adrian had been sadly disappointed. There was some evidence of progress during the first year, but Sir Adrian had then been outvoted at a Board meeting which had decided to transfer Scott-Air's Bahamian and Bermudan services to British Empire. The effect was that Scott-Air's operations would now be confined to low-density European routes. Sir Adrian belatedly realised that British Empire's interest all along had just been part of a plot to eliminate a growing competitor on its transatlantic routes,

Sir Adrian had then initiated another fund-raising exercise in order successfully to buy back the fifty-one precent shareholding. However, the development of Scott-Air had suffered a significant setback. It was only towards the end of the decade that Scott-Air had been able to start resuming wider international operations and replacing its outdated aircraft with second-hand all-jet Boeing 707s.

In 1969, the Government had commissioned a report by a Professor at the London School of Economics into the future of British civil aviation. The report had made a number of recommendations and had concluded that the independent airlines sector was too fragmented, and so there should be consolidation. The proposal was to create a "Second Force" Private Sector airline which would be financially and managerially strong and which would operate a state-of-the-art fleet. In order to achieve commercial viability, the Government would transfer certain current British Empire routes to the new entity.

McClean had seen this proposal as another opportunity to achieve what he had first attempted to do with Scott-Air in 1965. He immediately set about the task of Industry consolidation, and Government support was obtained for a number of mergers, led by Scott-Air. The result was a new airline which was to be known as Anglo-Scottish Airways. Operations had commenced in December 1970 with Adrian McClean as the Airline's Chief Executive. McClean's achievements were recognised by his nomination as Businessman of the Year in 1970. His knighthood had followed five years later, and Anglo-Scottish operations had steadily grown over the following decade. However, as Lawrence's research had revealed, recent times had become extremely tough.

Sir John buzzed through to Miss Palmer. "I am free now, and I should be grateful if you would ask Sir Adrian to join me."

Sir Adrian entered the lion's den. "Good afternoon, Sir John, and belated congratulations on your appointment at British International. Very well-deserved and hopefully you will be able to bring about some much-needed changes for the Industry".

"Thank you very much, Sir Adrian, and may we drop the Sirs?"

"Most certainly," said Sir Adrian. "I think the last time we met was as far back as the investiture ceremony, which, goodness me, is now more than ten years ago. How time flies."

"Yes, apologies that there has been such a long gap, but I have very much been looking forward to this meeting. Adrian, please take a seat at the big conference table over here. Now, how can I help you?"

"Well, John, I think it is really a case of us helping each other, but, of course, within the realms of fair competition and normal commercial practice. As you know, civil aviation is generally having quite a tough time at present. We, at Anglo-Scottish, are holding our own but, looking ahead, we feel the need to consolidate and to improve the quality and frequency of our long-haul route network. We are doing well in Europe and, of course, last year we placed our order for fifteen of the new Airbus A320s. We were the first non-French airline to order this aircraft. It will greatly improve efficiencies, and we anticipate considerable passenger interest."

Yes, thought Sir John, in the 1960s and 1970s British Empire had been constrained to "Buy British". As a result, it had, at times, operated a number of unsatisfactory domestically-produced aircraft types, not entirely suited to its requirements. Following the decline of the British civil aircraft manufacturing industry during the late 1970s, the Government had been forced to change its policy. It had then directed British Empire Airways to source all of its future new aircraft requirements from Boeing, which now also incorporated the Douglas commercial aircraft business.

Boeing was the preferred supplier because purchases from Airbus had effectively been banned because of its decision not to install Rolls-Royce engines in its first airliner, the A300. As a result of this decision, Rolls-Royce had been forced to go "cap in hand" to the American Lockheed Aircraft Corporation as being the only potential customer for its high technology RB211 turbofan engine. Lockheed had subsequently specified the RB211 to power its wide-bodied Tristar, but it had extracted stretching performance guarantees without conceding

45

any price improvements. There had then been development delays with the engine, leading to the bankruptcy of one of Britain's greatest and largest companies. The Government had effectively been forced to rescue the aero-engine business in 1971 and the company was still in Government hands.

Sir John would dearly like to order the A320 for British International and to let bygones be bygones with Airbus, but that was a discussion yet to be had with the Department of Trade and Industry.

Sir Adrian continued, "John, as you will no doubt recollect, the Government established Anglo-Scottish in order to provide the Nation with a sustainable Second Force Private Sector airline."

Sir Adrian opened his briefcase, extracted a document, and then proceeded to drop his bombshell.

"My colleagues and I at Anglo-Scottish have concluded that this objective can only be achieved if British International ceases its operations from Gatwick and transfers, to Anglo-Scottish, its Gatwick-based employees and aircraft together with the relevant routes. Here is a written proposal together with a list of some further routes which we consider should also properly be transferred to Anglo-Scottish in order to expand our Gatwick operations and to make them fully viable. If we are unable to expand at Gatwick, we might then need to consider initiating services from Heathrow. Of course, we would not expect British International to make these changes without appropriate financial compensation. My Board has considered the matter very seriously, and Anglo-Scottish proposes an initial payment of £100 million followed by a further, performance-related, £50 million payable over the next five years. What do you think?"

Sir John sat back, struggling to digest and assimilate Sir Adrian's proposal. Instead of the hoped for unconditional surrender, what he had just heard, he considered, could only be described as a "smash and grab raid!"

"Well, thank you very much, Adrian, for being so open and candid. I'm sure that we can do something together, but there is an awful lot to take in and to analyse. You will appreciate that I will need to have extensive discussions with my Executive colleagues and the Board before we can make any meaningful response. Also, the Department of Trade and Industry will need to be fully consulted."

"Of course, I fully understand that, Sir John, but time is pressing. We need to make these much-needed changes by the end of next year at the very latest."

"You may be assured, Adrian, that we will be giving your proposals our full attention."

Sir John rose from the conference table, indicating, with his body language, that the meeting was most definitely over. He steered Sir Adrian towards the door connecting with Miss Palmer's office. There was no reason to alert Sir Adrian to the existence of the escape door.

"Very nice to see you again, Adrian. I enjoyed our conversation, and I will be in touch with you as soon as possible."

Sir Adrian was able to complete his bowling conversation with Miss Palmer in the adjoining office before heading back down to the Anglo-Scottish Headquarters at Horley, next door to Gatwick.

"Miss Palmer, would you pop in please?" Sir John had, in his hand, the document presented by Sir Adrian.

"Would you please make a copy of this and then send it by courier to Mr Marshfield at Hounslow. Please enclose a short note asking him to take a read through and then to contact me with his initial views as soon as possible."

It had been quite a day. Perhaps now was the time for a relaxing evening. Unfortunately, it was not to be. He checked his "personal diary" to find an entry for one of Lady Eleanor's many social events. This time it was a fund-raising dance.

Sir John had so enjoyed dancing with his first wife, Laura, in their early years together. It was an opportunity to hold her tight and to whisper in her ear how much he loved her. Dancing with Lady Eleanor, like in most other activities, was very much more of a formal affair. However, the "deal" they had made upon their marriage in 1976 was that they would each support the other's business and social engagements. There was no question of opting out, much as he would very much like to have done on this and on many other previous occasions.

Harry Shining would not have any such issues. At this very moment, he would be well on his way back to Hove, where he would arrive in good time to be able to enjoy a relaxing evening at home.

Chapter 11
The Wisdom of Reggie

It was Friday of the same week, and the rotund, very affable, and now rapidly balding Reginald "Reggie" Joseph Laycock was looking forward to getting the day over and to then enjoying a relaxing weekend at his modestly-sized, but expensive, apartment adjacent to the bridge over the River Thames at Marlow. Reggie had been the Company Secretary of what was now British International Airlines for over ten years. A much-respected figure both within the company and also around the airline Industry generally, Reggie had started his career with British Empire Airways in the early 1950s, as a Junior Wages Clerk. He had studied and worked hard in order to aspire to his current senior position.

In his younger days, Reggie had been a reasonably successful goalkeeper in the Berkshire amateur football leagues, but those days were long gone. Reggie had since become a good, old-fashioned, confirmed bachelor. He had never had any strong inclinations towards marriage, and the opportunity had never arisen. He was very content with his professional life and with the small circle of friends whom he regularly entertained.

The Marlow apartment boasted Reggie's first pride and joy, a ridiculously-expensive, Poggenpohl kitchen equipped with equally expensive Miele appliances, in which he delighted in displaying his not inconsiderable culinary skills. Although not a great distance from Hounslow, the morning drive from Marlow was becoming more difficult, no matter what time Reggie left home. He loved his job, but the commuting issue was becoming increasingly negative.

His second pride and joy, his Jaguar XJS convertible, was of no benefit for this particular journey. Average speed was below thirty miles per hour, and the lusty engine consumed copious amounts of fuel as the traffic crawled along.

Overall, Reggie was glad to be edging slowly towards retirement, which was now just a few years away. He already had his retirement time well planned. He would continue to oversee the British International Final Salary Pension Scheme for two days a week, in the capacity of Managing Trustee. He would also preside over the Airline's Museum, which occupied a prime ground floor location at the Hounslow Headquarters and which he had been instrumental in setting up during the 1970s. The Museum now comprised a most important national archive, documenting the Country's civil aviation heritage from its inception in the 1920s.

On most of the remaining retirement days, he would take the XJS on a much more conducive five-mile drive along the Thames riverbank to the Phyllis Court Club at nearby Henley. Here he was the Secretary of the Aviation Interest Group, comprised of those many Club members who were retired former pilots or airline executives living in the Thames Valley area. The remainder of his time would be spent at the apartment, in the kitchen, and in watching the river traffic go by from his balcony.

During Sir John's first visit to the Hounslow Headquarters, following his appointment in June 1985, he had interviewed Reggie, who had passed the new Chairman's two evaluation tests with flying colours. During his subsequent monthly visits, it was to Reggie's office that Sir John invariably first made a beeline. Reggie was the person who could update him on the latest gossip and from whom he could find out exactly what was really going on in the company.

From his seat at the Board table for the last ten years, Reggie, with his bright twinkling eyes, had studied every Board Report which had been presented, making full use of his bifocal reading glasses, which were invariably perched precariously on the end of his nose. He consequently probably knew more about the Airline than any of its other Executives. The concise and elegant minutes that Reggie consistently produced, following those meetings, could be composed only with a thorough understanding of the details.

Lawrence had also recognised Reggie's value to the business, and so he had emulated Sir John in regularly calling by Reggie's office for informative chats. Reggie very much liked Lawrence Marshfield, the young and self-effacing new Chief Executive Officer. He was a refreshing change from his somewhat institutionalised predecessors. Reggie could not argue that others might consider him to be equally institutionalised. However, he had always tried to be reasonably outgoing. He was a member of a number of committees set up by the aviation industry's representative body, the International Air Transport Association (IATA). He was also the Airline's main point of contact with the Confederation of British Industry and was involved with the activities of the professional organisation for Company Secretaries.

Lawrence's reorganisation of the Executive Office, which he had mentioned to Miss Palmer, had created just five, glass-partitioned, cellular offices, accessed from a mid-sized general office area. Here, the work stations for the two secretaries/personal assistants were located. Four of the offices were occupied respectively by Lawrence, Reggie, the Group Finance Director, and the Head of Human Resources. The fifth office was available for use by the Chairman during his occasional visits. This morning, Lawrence was standing in the general office, and he beckoned to Reggie that he should join him for a meeting in his cellular office immediately.

"Good morning Reggie. If you have a moment, I would like a word about Anglo-Scottish Airways. The Chairman met with Sir Adrian McClean a few days ago, and Sir Adrian has made a proposal that Anglo-Scottish should acquire our Gatwick operations together with a number of our other routes. I have the formal proposal document here with all of the details, which I will copy and send over to you later."

Another of Reggie's talents was joke telling, together with a brilliant ability for mimicry. He had often employed these skills over the years to reduce tension in difficult situations.

51

"I am sure I will have some comments on Anglo-Scottish, Lawrence, but first I must tell you a new joke which I heard the other day. When I told it to Bob Graham, from our Insurance brokers, he was in absolute stitches."

"If you don't mind, Reggie, I think I'll take a rain check on the joke for the moment, if I may. Please save it for your spot at the next Board lunch. You know you have a very receptive audience. The Chairman, in particular, is a great fan of your jokes."

"Now, please let me have your initial thoughts on the Anglo-Scottish situation."

"As you wish, Lawrence." Reggie then adopted his best Scottish accent. "It seems to me, laddie, that Sir Adrian has had a wee bonny idea."

"What!" Lawrence gasped in horror and pushed his chair back from the desk.

Reggie hastened to placate the agitated Lawrence.

"Please do not worry Lawrence, seriously, it is definitely not a good idea. Just a little bit of my silly humour. Since you wouldn't let me tell my new joke, I thought I would make another attempt to amuse you."

"Well, that's a relief, please continue, Reggie, but preferably without the humour, just for the meantime at least."

"Seriously, Lawrence, it seems to me that Sir Adrian and Anglo-Scottish are definitely in deep trouble. I always have my ear to the ground, and the news on the street is that Anglo-Scottish is seeking to raise cash by selling some of its Caribbean hotels. I believe it has also just sold and leased back its fleet of BAC One Eleven twinjets. However, that transaction cannot have raised much cash because those aircraft are old, noisy, and dirty by current-day standards. New noise regulations will require them to be withdrawn in three years' time anyway. If matters become critical, it is possible that Anglo-Scottish might not be able to finance the fifteen Airbus A320s which it has on order. That would be an absolutely catastrophic situation for Sir Adrian."

Reggie continued.

"I think Anglo-Scottish can probably stagger on until the end of next year, but it will be curtains by early 1988 unless a white knight appears. In this regard, my sources tell me that Sir Adrian is courting a number of parties for possible salvation. Scandavia is believed to be one possible suitor, but of course, they are a State airline controlled by the Danish, Norwegian, and Swedish Governments. I cannot see our Conservative Government favouring an arrangement with them. Package Europe has also been rumoured, but, as the name suggests, they are mainly a holiday charter flight operation and so not really compatible with the ambition of Anglo-Scottish, which is to be predominantly a scheduled services operator. I am also advised that Package Europe is not in the best of financial situations."

"No doubt Sir Adrian is already in frequent contact with the Department of Trade and Industry, enlisting its support for a possible Anglo-Scottish rescue. He will also probably be lobbying for changes to the London Air Traffic Distribution Rules. These rules were brought in during the 1970s to place restrictions on the use of Heathrow and thereby improve the utilisation of Gatwick. Without modifications to the Rules, Anglo-Scottish is effectively confined to operating its London flights from Gatwick. I suspect that part of Sir Adrian's plan is to extend Anglo-Scottish operations to Heathrow, if his plan to acquire our Gatwick operations and those other routes proves to be unsuccessful."

"So what do you suggest we do then, Reggie?"

"Absolutely nothing. We should play for time over the next year and focus hard in the meantime on finalising our flotation plans. It seems to me that Sir Adrian has demonstrated that there are a number of conflicting issues between us and Anglo-Scottish Airways. If the Department of Trade and Industry wishes to make a successful British

International flotation happen, then it will have to make some difficult choices in early 1988 as to which of the two airlines it is going to back."

"Thank you for your assessment, Reggie, on the nail as usual. We should not be seen acting in a way so as to be accused of leading on Anglo-Scottish; however, it appears we have no alternative other than to ask Sir John to stall for as long as possible. I will make this request. Sir John is good at playing the political game; it is his forte."

Chapter 12
Lady Eleanor
and the Refurbishment

Time had subsequently moved on and it was now more than twelve months later, in the autumn of 1987. Sir John had suffered a very disturbed, late September, Monday night at the Belgravia apartment. He was alone because Lady Eleanor was at Bishop's Lake, orchestrating arrangements for the next weekend events in support of her bid for nomination as a Deputy Lieutenant of the County. He had therefore been able to enjoy an extra evening Havana corona, together with a couple of glasses of his favourite Brandy, before retiring to bed relatively early.

A noisy event was evidently in progress in the first-floor apartment above. In the early hours, as he lay asleep, Sir John was suddenly awakened from his nuptials by a loud crash. He was then deluged in broken plasterboard and splintered wood, as part of a sofa from the above apartment penetrated the ceiling and appeared, dangling dangerously and directly over the bed. Even worse, the sofa was alight and the fire was spreading very rapidly around the bedroom, with smoke circulating into other parts of the apartment. Despite his painful back, Sir John had made a very sprightly exit, just as the Fire Brigade was arriving. The Royal Lancaster Hotel was the nearest available refuge, and it was to there that he had relocated and spent what remained of the night.

The following morning, Lady Eleanor had received the news of the disaster with due concern. She was genuinely relieved to hear that Sir John was unscathed, but she could not help thoughts of a potential opportunity crossing her mind.

"So pleased to hear that you are unharmed, my dearest. The first thing now is to recover what remaining undamaged clothes there are at the apartment. Then get that lady who runs your office to move you from that dreadful hotel and into a suitable suite at Claridges for the meantime. Fortunately, I know there is a vacant Belgravia apartment, almost opposite ours. My friend, Fiona, who has recently parted from her awful husband, is now working for the Agency handling the letting. This apartment should be a suitable short-term replacement. Please ask the Company Secretary chappie at Hounslow, who I understand is responsible for properties, to put the wheels in motion for a six-month let; that should be sufficient for us. I will now contact Desmond Pollock."

"Very good, my dear, but I don't think I know a Mr Pollock."

"Oh, he is a most wonderful person and an absolute expert in interior design. He has worked for a number of friends, and he has also carried out some important projects for Royalty. I think it is essential that we have him involved as soon as possible."

Sir John cautiously acquiesced. In the overall scheme of things, he could not believe that the costs of the repairs to the apartment would be a major issue. Another aspect of his marriage deal with Eleanor was that they would live in a style commensurate with their position in Society.

Lady Eleanor Cresswell, formerly the Hon Eleanor Medway, was born in 1922 as the only child of an obscure Viscount, who had certainly experienced better financial days. The ever-diminishing family finances had stretched just far enough to allow Eleanor to attend a top, all-girls, Boarding School in Kent. She had left school with moderate academic achievements but with social skills of the highest order and including a very impressive list of future contacts.

The Second World War had then intervened, and Eleanor had found herself working in a clerical job at the War Ministry in Whitehall. In 1942, out of the blue, she received an official letter advising that she was being posted to a place called Bletchley Park. Apparently, this was some kind of Military facility further to the north of London than she had ever ventured or had ever wished to venture. It seemed the Military was looking for well-bred, middle-class girls, and Eleanor had definitely fitted the bill.

She had found herself billeted in a local Bedfordshire village, together with a number of other girls of similar age and background. Unexpectedly, it had all become rather good fun. The work itself was boring and repetitive, involving the confidential transit of large amounts of paper between various huts and then feeding cards into those noisy and ugly machines, which she had been told had been invented by a Mr Turing. She had seen him only infrequently, and she understood that he was now spending most of his time in America.

However, the Bletchley Park social life was excellent, with the opportunity to make even more useful connections. The highlight was the Amateur Dramatic Society. Eleanor had acted in a number of school productions, and she was a natural fit for many of the supporting roles. The Society put on a number of varied and well-received shows. It was a great disappointment to Eleanor when the war ended and everything had then come to an abrupt halt in the summer of 1945.

Sadly, Eleanor had lost both her parents during the last year of the war, when the family home in London had been destroyed, courtesy of a V1 Flying Bomb, part of Hitler's final effort to salvage Germany from the inevitable final defeat. With what remained of the family assets, Eleanor had been able to purchase a modest flat off Kensington High Street and to enrol herself on a Le Cordon Bleu culinary and hospitality course, in order to enhance her already excellent social skills. She had then set up a small hospitality services company and had developed a loyal clientele amongst small banks and professional firms. Her "meet and greet" skills were second to none, and she very rarely lost any clients.

Eleanor had discovered that she had limited or no maternal instincts, although she had accepted invitations to become godmother to more children than she could now easily remember. She was not averse to male company, but, as an independent woman who had made her way in the world, she was not actively looking for a husband. She had met the newly-knighted Sir John, in late 1975, at an event which she had organised for a merchant banking client. Sir John had been single then for just over ten years and was similarly not actively looking for a new partner. However, he had found himself attracted to this tall and graceful woman, now in her mid-fifties and clearly very well socially connected.

Separately, Eleanor had decided that she had taken her business as far as she wished or as was reasonably feasible. The London scene was consolidating, many of her clients were merging, and, in some cases, they were going out of business. The offer of marriage from Sir John was unexpected, but she had given it considerable thought. She had concluded that there was definitely a strong liking between the two of them, possibly not love, but that they would be able to rub along well together. So she had decided to accept Sir John's offer and also to transfer her client list to an emerging large hospitality group. She had then wound up her own business with sufficient funds, from the client list transfer, now available in the bank to deal with any unforeseen future disasters.

The marriage took place quietly at the Kensington and Chelsea Register Office in early 1976. The deal between the newly weds was that they would provide mutual support for their respective activities. Eleanor had no intention of foregoing her "London Life," but this suited Sir John with his ongoing aspirations for ascendancy into The British Establishment. The availability of Bishop's Lake for weekends was a definite plus and would enable Eleanor to create a whole new County-level social network. The two had never subsequently questioned or doubted the wisdom of their union.

A few weeks before the marriage, there had been a Cresswell family conference with lawyers present. Sir John was determined that there would be no arguments over the "Cresswell dynasty" following his death. The lawyers stated that their instructions were to transfer the majority of Sir John's assets into a Family Investment Company. In 1970, the Midlands & West Group had become a public company. Sir John had then sold most of his shares in the Company, whilst retaining a strategic five percent holding. The proceeds of the 1970 share sales had been used to create a substantial investment portfolio. This portfolio, together with the residual shareholding in the Midlands & West Group, would now be transferred to the Family Investment Company.

Sir John would have no entitlement to the income or assets of the Family Investment Company and each of Eleanor and the three children would have a twenty-five percent interest. In addition, the children and Lady Eleanor would each immediately receive payment of an index-linked monthly allowance of £2,000. Eleanor would be entitled to the remainder of Sir John's estate upon his death, and she would have the right to reside at Bishop's Lake for her lifetime. If she decided to sell the property, then the proceeds would be split four ways. The lawyers were instructed to register a Restriction against the Title of Bishop's Lake in respect of a right of access to be granted to the mounded area. This right provided for members of the Cresswell family and their maintenance contractors to have unrestricted access, in perpetuity, to the two burial plots.

All present had appeared to be content with the financial arrangements, although Eleanor had felt privately that she should be entitled to receive all of the proceeds of the eventual sale of Bishop's Lake. The children seemed happy with their proposed allowances. Andrew was the most enthusiastic, of course. Robert appeared reluctant, although he did not refuse. Sir John suspected that Robert would not mention this additional income source to his socially-active wife. He would probably use the allowance to supplement his moderate profit-share from the Tunbridge Wells legal practice. His total income would then appear to be not quite so low when compared with the profit shares of the City-based lawyers living in the neighbourhood. However most of them would be burnt out by their early fifties, whilst Robert was antic-ipating that he would enjoy a much longer and considerably less stress-ful career.

Sir John's daughter, Sandra, who was now married to a House Mas-ter teaching Classics at a West Country Public School, said that she had no idea what to do with the allowance. She was earning a perfectly reasonable salary as Deputy Head of the School's Preparatory Section. They were living on site, and all three of their children would soon be pupils at the school, with heavily discounted fees. She would "probably put the money in the bank" and perhaps give some to charity. Sir John had no issues with reasonable charitable donations, but winced at the prospect of his money lingering in the bank, earning only cursory in-terest. However, he accepted that Sandra was not one of the world's natural entrepreneurs and that her academic husband was even less so inclined.

Chapter 13
A Negotiation

It was just over three weeks since the Chairman's escapade in the Belgravia apartment. Reggie's team had negotiated the suggested six-month lease of the apartment opposite, which, fortunately, was fully furnished. Reggie had struggled into work early this morning because he was expecting some visitors. Despite his early start, Friday traffic on the way to Hounslow seemed to become ever more challenging. Reggie's Jaguar XJS had consumed even more than its usual quantity of high-octane petrol on the tedious stop-start journey.

Reggie was advised that his visitors had arrived slightly early. He had barely risen from his chair before Lady Cresswell, power-suited in Jaeger and crowned with a pillbox hat, surged into his office. A diminutive figure was trailing in her wake, partially hidden by the large portfolio case which the said individual was carrying.

"Good morning, your ladyship, how nice to see you again."

"Good morning to you also, Mr Laycock. Thank you for your help so far in sorting out this awful mess."

Reggie assumed that the said "awful mess" was the Belgravia apartment fire affair.

"May I introduce you to Desmond Pollock?"

The diminutive figure emerged from behind the portfolio case. He was clad in a well-tailored blue blazer, with light grey flannels, and wearing a pastel shirt with a toning bow tie and pocket handkerchief. He had delicate features, and there was a good head of carefully styled hair, clearly dyed and now greying slightly. Reggie estimated that he must be in his mid-fifties.

"Good morning, Mr Laycock". Said the figure, then turning to her ladyship and enquiring, "Would you like me to produce the designs?" Pollock moved to open his portfolio case, but before Lady Cresswell could answer, the intercom buzzed with the message that another visitor had arrived.

"Lady Cresswell, I took the liberty of inviting Bob Graham, the Account Director from our Insurance Brokers, to attend this meeting. I hope you have no objection. It seemed to me that getting him involved now should save time later."

"I entirely agree, most sensible Mr Laycock. Please ask Mr Graham to join us."

The well-presented Bob Graham had spent his entire working life in Insurance Broking and had managed to maintain continuity of employment with the company, which, after a series of mergers and amalgamations, had eventually emerged as the American-owned, Whishaw Inc. Bob, now in his late fifties, was a daily commuter into the City from his home in Benfleet, Essex. It was then a very short walk from Fenchurch Street Station, across Trinity Square, to the rather grand Headquarters which Whishaw Inc. had inherited from one of its traditional British-owned Insurance Broker predecessors. During his morning train journeys, Bob would read the Daily Telegraph from cover to cover. He was consequently remarkably well-informed on current affairs. This fund of knowledge was invaluable in facilitating small talk with clients, both prospective and actual.

The British International Airlines Insurance account was very extensive, covering aircraft, employees, liability, and, of course, properties, one of which was the dreaded Belgravia apartment. British International was amongst Whishaw Inc.'s top five clients in the UK, and Bob considered himself honoured to have the responsibility of managing this most prestigious of accounts. He was also certainly at pains to ensure that nothing occurred, which might either tarnish his reputation or potentially prejudice his promised early retirement package from Whishaw Inc. at age sixty.

Bob Graham entered the room. Lady Cresswell strode over towards Reggie's conference table, beckoning the three males to join her, whilst directing Pollock to produce the contents of his portfolio bag.

"Desmond has done such a wonderful job in setting out plans for the complete restoration of the apartment. He has been there almost every day, and his involvement has been of great personal comfort and support to me and to Sir John over the past traumatic weeks. I know that Sir John has taken a personal interest in the matter and has been most impressed with Desmond's efforts."

Desmond then laid his plans on the table. They indicated the necessary structural repairs, together with details of an associated complete redecoration of the entire apartment. There were also a number of proposed modifications to the internal layout and a long list of proposed replacement furnishings.

Reggie and Bob studied the plans with growing alarm. Reggie decided to let Bob do most of the talking.

"Very interesting, your ladyship," observed Bob. "I just have one main comment, which is that the Insurance Policy conditions, of course, only provide for reinstatement and not for any improvement or enhancement aspects. My understanding was that the damage was contained primarily to the main bedroom and that most of the remainder of the apartment and its furnishings were completely unscathed."

Lady Cresswell stiffened in her chair and focused her gaze on the unfortunate Insurance Executive.

"I do think you are taking a rather bureaucratic and, I must say, a most unfair approach. What's your name again? Oh yes, of course, Mr Graham."

"Mr Graham, you must realise that this affair has been a major intrusion into the lives of Sir John and me. Sir John's life was put at risk, and we have been evicted from our home, which no longer feels to be our own. It needs to be completely renewed, and it is essential that Desmond's plans are implemented quickly and without variation. Some normality can then be returned to our lives."

A flustered Bob responded. "Your ladyship, I very much understand the upset, and I can completely sympathise with your situation, but I feel it is necessary to specify what the insurance covers and what it does not. However, I suggest we move on for the moment and perhaps look at the costings. Provided these are within reasonable parameters, then this should reduce the risks of the Insurers denying the claim. I assume that Mr Pollock has some indicative figures?"

Desmond did indeed have some figures which he proceeded to extract from his bag and which were then placed in front of Bob and Reggie. The costs of the repairs, changes to layout, and re-decoration were £350,000, together with around £250,000 for furniture replacement.

Desmond Pollock then commented, "Of course, there is, in addition, my twenty percent commission. Also, we always have a substantial contingency fund, which usually seems to be very necessary. I think that Sir John and her ladyship's living arrangements can be restored to their proper and appropriate level for a total budget of around £800,000. We need to press on with the work now."

The blood had drained from Bob's face. He had entered the meeting with a maximum budget figure in his head for the entire apartment restoration of around £300,000.

Reggie decided it was time for him to contribute. "Mr Pollock, clearly, we cannot give the go-ahead now, and I would also like to query the redecoration costs. We recently carried out a large refurbishment here at Hounslow with very satisfactory results. I would suggest obtaining an alternative quote for that part of the work from the British International decoration contractors."

Desmond rolled his eyes.

"Mr Laycock, it is essential that only my decorators are used."

Pollock had placed strong emphasis on the word "my".

"I will not otherwise engage in or put my name to a project."

Lady Cresswell vigorously nodded her head in agreement. Reggie's suggestion was a definite non-starter. The meeting was coming to a rapid close. Desmond scrambled to gather up his papers, whilst leaving a copy of the costings for Bob and Reggie to deliberate over. Lady Cresswell swept out of the room, with Desmond Pollock trailing behind. Her parting words were:

"Thank you very much for your time, gentlemen. Sir John is, of course, being kept fully informed about progress, and I very much hope that the go-ahead will be given next week, without any unnecessary delay."

Lady Cresswell and Desmond Pollock departed. Reggie asked his secretary to arrange for two much-needed cups of strong coffee. Reggie related his latest joke to Bob, who was soon convulsed with laughter and was now steadily recovering some of his composure.

Reggie said. "Well, in the overall scheme of things, Bob, where British International pays around £25 million of premiums for its annual insurance programme, I would have thought that there is some scope for manoeuvre here, what do you think?"

"Reggie, that is possibly the case, but not the difference of £500,000 between my £300,000 estimate and the £800,000 costings of our friend, Mr Pollock. I might be able to get the Insurers up to £500,000, but that still leaves a difference of £300,000."

"Fine, I suggest you proceed on that basis, Bob. With regard to the difference, I propose we share it 50:50. I am aware that we both hold a reserve fund, which it seems we must now respectively utilise. My department will be responsible for authorising Pollock's bills, and we will certainly ensure that his so-called contingency fund remains intact and unused. Also, any furnishings acquired will be owned by British International, whatever her ladyship might think. So there will, at least, be some residual value for the Corporation there."

Bob Graham left Reggie's office, still shaken, but most impressed with Reggie's sharp analysis and proposed pragmatic solution to the problem. He could now see a way forward which, hopefully, would jeopardise neither Whishaw Inc.'s stewardship of the British International account nor, more importantly, his retirement plans. He would be fully focused on implementing Reggie's solution, assuming that Reggie could persuade the Airline's Chief Executive Officer to approve it.

Chapter 14
Flotation Issues

Later on that Friday morning, Lawrence called by at Reggie's office.

"Good morning Reggie. Was that Lady Cresswell I saw you with earlier? What is she up to, and who was that rather odd-looking chap running around after her?"

"Yes, Lawrence, I have just recovered from a rather difficult meeting with her ladyship. Her companion was an apparently well-known interior designer whom she has roped in to oversee the Belgravia apartment damage repairs. I can update you now on where we are, if you like."

Reggie summarised the events of the meeting and reported his proposed pragmatic apartment renovation financial solution. Lawrence thought deeply and sighed:

"So it looks as though we are between a rock and a hard place. I will go along with your proposal, Reggie, but I am not going to tolerate any kind of cover-up. Any amounts that we cannot properly recover from the Insurers must be recorded and fully disclosed as uninsured losses. If the Corporation's followers in the Financial community pick them up, then so be it. We will just have to tough it out. As you have said, at least the new furnishings will be owned by us. So we will have something to show when they are acquired and are then included as Fixed Assets in the Balance Sheet."

"Thank you, and quite correct if I may say, Lawrence. I should also mention that the apartment lease has a break clause enabling us to terminate it early in the autumn of 1990. I am assuming that Sir John will be lobbying strongly for a second five-year term as Chairman, in which case we will not exercise the break and will allow the lease to run for its full term to the autumn of 1995. However, if by any chance Sir John does not continue, then we will terminate the lease, and we should be able to recoup some of the refurbishment costs by selling the furnishings."

"Excellent summary, Reggie, and so we will proceed on this basis. Whilst I am here, please update me on how we are getting on with the main flotation tasks?"

"Well, as you know, Lawrence, with regard to the updating of the aircraft fleet, we are now receiving the new Boeing 757s, which were ordered by your predecessor. We are using them to phase out the trijet Hawker Siddeley Tridents, which have served us well but which are now very definitely time-expired. We are progressively replacing the One Elevens with Boeing 737s, but we could really do with some A320s. One benefit of a deal with Anglo-Scottish would be to get our hands on the fifteen they have ordered and which will be delivered next year. Ever since Anglo-Scottish placed its A320 order, which was much-appreciated by Airbus, a flurry of interest has been generated in the aircraft. We would now be behind a long queue of purchasers if we placed an order ourselves."

"OK Reggie, I see you did not mention the Subsonic Cruiser issue. I think this situation is also a definite concern, but I suggest we leave it for review towards the end of the year. Can we move on to people issues, please?"

"This is not really my area, Lawrence, but as I understand it from Human Resources, we need to reduce employment numbers by fifteen thousand. It is not going to be easy, and the Unions will no doubt cut up rough. Part of our pre-flotation negotiations with the Department should include the provision of assistance towards the funding of a major redundancy plan."

Reggie continued:

"One area where I am very much involved is the pensions situation. Being a State-owned corporation since the end of the war, it has not been possible to offer significant bonuses or share-based incentives in order to retain key employees. The main retention benefit, therefore, has been through the use of the Final Salary Pension Scheme. Accordingly, we have made the Scheme about as generous as a pension scheme can be. It has a very high annual accrual rate and excellent early retirement arrangements. For example, pilots and flight engineers can elect to retire at any age from fifty onwards without any reduction in their pensions."

"Yes, I am well aware of the early retirement benefits," said Lawrence. "I understand that quite a large number of pilots and flight engineers are currently taking advantage of them and then joining our competitors. Sir John will be absolutely livid when he finds out. Do you have a plan to solve the pensions issue?"

"Yes, and, in a word, it is closure. Apart from the Scheme's excessively generous benefits, the funding costs are going through the roof. This is very annoying because the Actuarial Profession generally clearly failed to recognise adequately the combined effects of increasing member longevity and weaker investment returns. The Scheme is already in deficit, and the situation will only get worse the longer that it remains open. When I say closure, I mean, of course, closure to new entrants and to future accrual. Current members will keep their benefits earned so far, but, for the future, they will have to move to a replacement Money Purchase Scheme. The investment risk under this type of scheme is placed on the members, and there is no pension promise underwritten by the sponsoring company. Another chunk of funding will be required from the Government to ensure that, at flotation, the liabilities already accrued under the Final Salary Pension Scheme are secured for the long term by purchasing suitable matching investments."

"Right," said Lawrence. "It seems Human Resources certainly has its work cut out, but so be it. Still some time left to formulate our detailed flotation plans, but where actions can be initiated in the meantime, we should get on with them. When we present our final flotation proposals early next year, we need to be able to demonstrate that good progress has already been made."

"Whilst we are talking about pensions, Lawrence, I should also mention that I am personally a member of the Scheme's top benefits tier. As a result, I am in the fortunate position of being able to choose to retire at any time from now on, whereupon I would receive the maximum Inland Revenue-permitted pension."

"Well, Reggie, I hope you are not thinking of retiring before the projected flotation."

Reggie replied. "I fully intend to be around for the flotation and for up to a year afterwards. Assuming all goes to plan, I will then bow out in early 1990, when I will be sixty. Meanwhile, you will have my full support, and hopefully, my knowledge and experience will be of value."

Lawrence knew that Reggie's support, knowledge, and experience would indeed be invaluable in the challenging period ahead.

Chapter 15
The Corporate Raider

For Miss Jennifer Palmer, the summer of 1987 at the Midlands & West Group had, so far, passed by rather quietly. At the behest of Lady Eleanor, Sir John had been away for a month, from mid-July to mid-August. One of Lady Eleanor's close friends had insisted that the couple should join her at her splendid residence at Antibes on the French Côte d'Azur. Miss Palmer had the distinct impression that Sir John was not particularly keen on the idea. He was not a sun-seeker, but, as usual, he had felt obliged to comply with his second wife's wishes.

The high-powered couple had departed across the English Channel in the "Roller" with Gerry chauffeuring. An overnight stop had been made at Lyon, together with a number of other necessary stops for refuelling purposes. The Roller's limited range was another black mark for Rolls-Royce Motors so far as Sir John was concerned. Gerry was not at all bothered. He had not been able to believe his luck. A months' holiday in the sun and on full pay to boot!

Serious trouble at the Midlands & West Group had emerged in mid-August. The Group was scheduled to announce its Preliminary Results for the year ended 31 May 1987 at the end of the month. The Accounts preparation process had followed its normal course, but, at a very late stage, one of the bright young things in Finance had unearthed and had passed to the Auditors a Consultant's Report on a Water Treatment plant project. The Group was currently engaged in constructing this plant in Saudi Arabia. The project had been underway for some years, but it was far behind schedule. One of the issues that was limiting progress was a lack of adequate raw water supplies to treat!

The standard accounting practice, for long-term projects of this nature, and which had been followed so far for the purposes of the

71

Water Treatment plant project, was to assess progress each year and then to make an appropriate credit or debit to the Profit & Loss Account. The remaining ongoing project work would be categorised as an asset and then reported as Work in Progress in the Balance Sheet.

Earlier in the year, Mike Holland had commenced a troubleshooting assessment of the Saudi Arabian project and had commissioned the Consultant's Report. He had also authorised significant further expenditure in an attempt to put the project back on track. His rationale was that the Saudi's would then have no excuse for refusing further stage payments.

The Consultant's Report had not been optimistic. It had been disclosed that the initial site surveys had been inadequate and the processing technology was outdated. The Report had concluded that there were no reasonable prospects of the plant ever achieving the specified performance. Mike Holland had passed the Report to the Midlands & West Finance Director, assuming, in good faith, that the appropriate Accounting actions would be taken. The Finance Director had quietly buried the Report in the pious hope that the situation would somehow improve.

The Auditors were now correctly demanding that the previous credits to Profit & Loss must be reversed, together with the writing off of the remaining value of the Work in Progress from the Balance Sheet. In addition, the further amounts authorised by Mike Holland in his efforts to rescue the project also needed to be written off and charged to Profit & Loss. The consequence of this Accounting failure was that the Accounts would have to be restated. The effect was a £7.5 million hit to the Profit and Loss figure for the Financial Year to 31 March 1987.

Estimated performance figures for the Year had previously been indicated to the Market, and The Stock Exchange had already been advised of the scheduled date for the issue of the Preliminary Results. To allow for the necessary additional accounting and audit work, this date now had to be moved back by two weeks. The release of this disturbing news to the Market, particularly the reduced profit figure, had exacerbated what was an already steep decline in the Midlands & West Group share price.

Upon hearing of the disaster, following his return from the Côte d'Azur, an enraged Sir John had flung open the escape door and had charged out of his office and down the corridor heading towards the Finance Director's office, where the poor incumbent was cowering behind the desk. However, by the time he reached the office, some calm had been restored in Sir John's mind. He had concluded that a shouting match would be of no benefit. The offences were not criminal, although summary termination of the employment contract would be both fully merited and supportable. He decided to suspend the individual, who would return after a week's rest, in order to assist the Auditors in completing the revised Accounts. The individual would present them at the Annual General Meeting in the normal manner. Enough damage had already been done without the further embarrassment of a wide public disclosure that the company was without a Finance Director.

Once the Annual General Meeting was out of the way, the Finance Director would serve out the remainder of his contractual notice on gardening leave. He would then be able to claim his pension, but there would be no enhancement. The standard Actuarial practice would be applied to reduce the amount payable by four percent for every year of early payment, prior to the normal retirement date. Privately, Sir John had had a twinge of guilt that he might have put too much pressure on the Finance Director. He was also now worried that his recent preoccupations with the affairs of British International Airlines might have been to the detriment of the well-being of the Midlands & West Group.

Having recently narrowly survived his near-death experience in the Belgravia burning apartment incident, Sir John now had another difficult task, which was to navigate the Midlands & West Group through its Annual General Meeting, to be held in early October. At the said meeting, Sir John had needed all of his experience and charisma in order to parry a number of difficult questions from analysts and investors and to fend away the most determined interrogators.

He was now thinking that he must allocate his working time more equitably. But in the second week of October, this thought process was suspended when Miss Palmer buzzed through on the intercom.

"There is a Mr Richard Hansard on the line, Sir John. Do you wish to take the call?"

"Yes, by all means, Miss Palmer, please put him through."

Sir John had been jolted into a state of high alert, and he had become icy cold. Richard Hansard was a well-known "Corporate Raider," and he was the Chairman of the Hansard Group. The term "Corporate Raider" had first been coined in America, where it had been discovered that under-performing companies could be taken over using highly leveraged loans secured against the prospective future cash flows from the acquisition target. Once in control, the Corporate Raider would realise value by breaking up the acquired company on the principle that the collective value of its parts was significantly greater than the whole. Richard Hansard was the leading exponent of the technique in the UK, and he had built up a large conglomerate. Annoyingly, the upstart Hansard had become a darling of the City, much feted in the Press and with a much higher public profile than that of Sir John.

"Good morning Richard, how nice to speak with you."

"Likewise, Sir John. I will get straight down to business. Have you been watching your share price recently?"

"Most certainly, it took a bit of a wobble after that minor issue with the Accounts, but it has since been recovering strongly. This trend has been very good to see."

"May I ask if you have been monitoring your Share Register?"

"That is something which I delegate to the Finance Director, and nothing in particular has been reported to me. Why do you ask?" Sir John already knew the answer to his question.

"I have to tell you, Sir John, that the Hansard Group has been steadily purchasing Midlands & West Group shares in the market over the last month, using a number of nominee accounts. The increase in your share price is entirely down to the demand we have created. We have now accumulated a holding of nearly thirty percent. I will be quite frank. You either recommend an agreed bid to your shareholders, or the Hansard Group will make a hostile tender for the remainder of your share capital. What is your choice?"

"Richard, I think that all of this proposal is rather sudden. You cannot possibly expect an immediate response. My obvious question is what price would you be offering to acquire the shares that you do not already hold?"

"The price will be ten percent over today's market price."

"But the share price was far higher than that twelve months ago. The normal premium for this kind of deal is around forty percent of market price on the day of the bid."

Hansard responded. "The City's current perception of the Midlands & West Group is that it is moribund, with significant value to be realised through a new management approach. I am very confident that we will have the required support for a hostile bid, at the price I have stated, if that becomes necessary."

Moribund and a new management approach indeed, Sir John bristled. What Hansard was suggesting was nothing less than a cheap takeover followed by a crude demolition of the business that he and Laura had painstakingly built up over so many years. What would Laura think? She would be horrified and would doubtless give him a hard time that his preoccupations with British International might have contributed to this sad state of affairs.

"Richard, I really think we have taken matters as far as we can in this conversation. What is your timescale?"

"We are governed by The Stock Market rules, and it is important that the risks of speculation are minimised. We need a response within the next forty-eight hours. Otherwise, our tender will be launched before the end of this month."

The call ended, and Sir John sat back with mixed feelings. After so many years of acquiring and rationalising under-performing businesses, albeit with funds properly accumulated from manufacturing and trading activities, it now seemed that the boot was on the other foot. Realistically, the likelihood of being able to fend off a hostile bid would be low, and significant costs would be involved. The best that could be achieved would be some improvement in the takeover price and possibly a number of pre-takeover changes designed to improve the position of the employees. After all, Sir John had a conscience. There would be many job losses, and the first item on the hit list would be the Corporate Office.

Sir John immediately arranged to convene with his various advisers. They had confirmed his assessment. Sir John rapidly came to terms with the fact that to fight on would be hopeless. At least he would no longer have to worry about allocating his future time, and he would be able to focus his efforts entirely on British International.

Appropriate consultations had then been conducted by The Midlands & West Group's merchant bankers with leading shareholders, and it was clear that there was support for the Hansard proposal. The Midlands & West Group Board had been convened and had authorised the bankers to respond positively to the Hansard Group and to negotiate final terms. Sir John had no wish to re-engage personally with its cocky Chairman.

A takeover share price of twelve percent over the current market value was then agreed, with the understanding that a pre-takeover payment of £50 million would be made to the M&W Group Final Salary

Pension Scheme in order to create a surplus which was to be used to protect accrued pensions rights and to fund early retirements. A Stock Market announcement was then made that, subject to shareholder approval, which would be just a formality, the Midlands & West Group would become part of the Hansard Group with effect from 1 January 1988. The reality was that the Midlands & West Group would largely cease to exist on that date. Its constituent parts would either be sold off or closed or would be merged into compatible businesses within the Hansard Group, in the limited instances where such compatibility existed.

Chapter 16
Final Flotation Preparations

The following months were busy, and Sir John had had little time to dwell on the sad Midlands & West Group debacle; it was now just a matter of dealing with the remaining issues to enable the takeover of the Group to be completed on schedule.

British International Airlines needed to agree on its final flotation strategy, which was scheduled to be presented to the Department of Trade and Industry in January 1988. The British International team, led by Lawrence and Reggie, had been working on flotation issues for over a year now, and there had been many joint meetings with representatives of the Department of Trade and Industry.

However, a very serious operational incident over the October school half term break had then brought about a new perspective on matters. A relatively new British International Boeing 737 had been chartered to fly a group of holiday makers from Manchester to the Greek island of Corfu. The aircraft had one hundred and thirty-one passengers on board, together with a crew of six. During the course of its take-off run there had been an explosion in the aircraft's port engine. Hot debris from the stricken engine penetrated the wing and ignited fuel then started to gush from a damaged fuel tank.

The highly-experienced co-pilot, who was in control, managed to abort the take-off run and to bring the aircraft to a halt at the side of the runway. By this time the fire was spreading rapidly and the cabin of the aircraft was beginning to fill with toxic fumes. After a struggle, the Purser and Stewardess working at the front of the aircraft managed to open the two front doors and to activate the escape shoots. The rear of the aircraft was now engulfed in flames and so it was not feasible to open the rear doors.

There were then delays in releasing the emergency escape hatches which allowed passengers to exit from the cabin and on to the wings of the aircraft. Panic-stricken passengers at the rear of the aircraft attempted to move forward towards these exits but many were overcome by fumes. Exit routes rapidly became blocked by the bodies of passengers who had collapsed and, in many cases, who had died during their attempts to escape. Airport fire engines were quickly on the scene, but the fire was too fierce to enable firemen to gain access in order to rescue passengers from the cabin.

The news of this dreadful incident was quickly communicated to Hounslow. Lawrence and Reggie had immediately raced up to Manchester Airport in order to take control of events, so far as practicable, and to deal with the media and with the relevant authorities.

The sad reality had then emerged that fifty-three of the passengers together with two members of the crew had died. Lawrence and Reggie remained in Manchester for three days and ensured that appropriate counselling was made available to bereaved families. The two pilots had survived the incident but the Captain was so traumatised that he would never again fly passengers.

An initial enquiry had absolved the airline from any culpability, but the incident would lead to future Industry changes on procedures for aircraft evacuations. Emergency floor lighting would be a requirement together with changes in aircraft seat layouts, also in the materials used for aircraft seat construction. Lawrence had immediately instructed that the row of seats adjacent to the two wing exits should be removed from all British International 737s until the revised and safer internal seat layouts were introduced by the manufacturer.

The cabin crew members were subsequently awarded the Queen's Gallantry Medal for their heroic and selfless efforts to save life. Sadly it was necessary for these awards to be made posthumously in the case of the two Stewardesses at the rear of the aircraft, who had perished in the course of their valiant attempts to evacuate passengers.

It was with this shocking incident still front of mind that, in early December 1987, Lawrence and Reggie were now convened with Sir John in his office at Hounslow.

"First may I express my appreciation to you both and to the rest of the British International team for the considerate and compassionate manner in which the Manchester Airport incident was managed. Also for the Industry-leading actions which you have initiated on behalf of British International." Said Sir John.

"We are, of course, nevertheless obligated to proceed with the flotation of the Airline, but let us take this tragic event as being a reminder of the magnitude of the risks and responsibilities that we bear in running an airline of the size of British International."

Lawrence and Reggie agreed with Sir John's comments and thanked him for his kind and appropriate words.

Lawrence now proceeded with the business of the meeting for which he had prepared a number of financial schedules on his Personal Computer. To Sir John's amazement, he had somehow managed to display them on a large wall-mounted screen in the office. This was certainly not an ability within the skill set of the ill-fated, Midlands & West Group Finance Director who had recently departed the company. After the financial update from Lawrence, the three Executives had received presentations from the Operations Team on route profitability and on aircraft fleet performance and replacement.

After a short lunch break, Human Resources, then reported the steady progress being made in reducing over-manning. Reggie then outlined a new Money Purchase Pension Scheme to be introduced on 1 June 1988, with the existing Final Salary Pension Scheme being closed to new members and to future accrual from that date. The proposal was to make the closure announcement early next year, and there would be some transitional arrangements, including the introduction of Company-paid enhanced life insurance for members of the new Scheme.

It had already been a long day. In the late afternoon and, following a tea break, Lawrence and Reggie had reconvened with Sir John.

"Well, I must say that I am most impressed," said Sir John. "The progress we have made over the past year is very encouraging, but there are clearly some remaining trouble spots. I would like to gain a better understanding of these critical issues. First, where are we with Anglo-Scottish? I have been putting off a second meeting with Sir Adrian, now for well over a year, and I simply cannot prevaricate for much longer."

Lawrence indicated for Reggie to respond.

"Yes, Sir John, as you will recollect, we forecast back in the spring of 1986 that Anglo-Scottish Airways was in for a difficult time. The grapevine confirms that revenue is down, losses are deepening, and that Sir Adrian is getting increasingly desperate. He has been lobbying very widely, and he is regularly in and out of the Department of Trade and Industry. I believe that the President of the Board of Trade, Lord Avonmouth, has been persuaded to instruct the Civil Aviation Authority to analyse current route allocations and to report on the proposals which Sir Adrian previously made to you. We think Anglo-Scottish must now be very close to the brink."

Sir John commented.

"Ah, yes, Lord Avonmouth, I have had the pleasure of meeting him at a few events. Another pompous Oxbridge type, if ever there was one. He has never worked a proper day in his life, in my opinion. Not actually producing anything, but just creating wealth, primarily for himself, simply through fly-by-night property speculation. Most undeserving of his elevation to the peerage, in my view. However, he is no fool and is clearly still very ambitious for the top job. Fortunately, I do not envisage the Prime Minister standing aside for the foreseeable future. I suspect his lordship wishes to be seen to be taking British civil aviation into what he perceives to be a new era. He will then pose as being its saviour and seek to emerge in a blaze of glory. We need to ensure that his ambitions do not conflict with the best interests of British International."

Sir John continued.

"If the Department is awaiting the CAA Report on Anglo-Scottish, then it seems I still have one final excuse to delay, yet again, a follow-up meeting with Sir Adrian. I can say that we cannot meet until the Report has been received and we have discussed its implications."

Lawrence responded

"I concur, Sir John. Absolutely the correct course of action. Hopefully, you can put off Sir Adrian for just a little longer."

"Now, I suggest we move on to pre-flotation funding. We need to agree with the Department on an appropriate contribution to the British International redundancy plan and also a once-off payment into the Final Salary Pension Scheme. We also need to discuss the issue of the Supersonic Cruiser. Reggie is very familiar with this saga, and perhaps he can fill in the background."

Reggie asked. "Would you like me to summarise the past history as well, very briefly, Sir John?"

"Yes, please, Reggie," said Sir John. "I know the broad outline, but an inside track would be most useful."

Reggie proceeded, "In 1962, the British and French Governments signed a Treaty for the production of a Supersonic Transport, the SST. The work was to be split 50:50 between the two countries, with the two primary British contractors, the British Aircraft Corporation and Bristol Siddeley Engines, carrying out most of the British development work at their Bristol facilities."

"Sorry to interrupt, Reggie, but wasn't Lord Avonmouth one of the Bristol MPs before his elevation to the peerage?"

"Indeed, Sir John, and that may be something to bear in mind."

"Please continue, Reggie."

"The SST project was at the very leading edge of technology, and the aircraft did not fly until 1969. British Empire Airways was not particularly keen on the idea of flying supersonic, and one of your predecessors described the aircraft as "being an infernal nuisance." As you can imagine, this comment did not go down too well at the time with the Government. That particular individual's term of office was not extended!"

"The sonic booms produced when the SST passed through the sound barrier, together with the noise it created during take-off and landing, became major issues. The American, Indian, and Malaysian Governments resorted to International Law in order to ban supersonic flights over their respective countries, which was a killer blow for the SST. Both sponsoring Governments were highly embarrassed, and there was then a major redesign exercise. All of those foreign airlines that had previously expressed interest in the SST were then able to drop their purchase options, without liability.

"The redesign would produce a fundamentally different aircraft to be called the Subsonic Cruiser which aircraft did not emerge until 1975. Sonic booms were then no longer a concern because, as its name suggests, the aircraft was incapable of flying supersonic. Instead, it cruises at just below the speed of sound. Take-off and landing noise, however, has been a continuing problem, and it was not until the early 1980s that commercial services could be established. Only ourselves and Air France, being owned by the British and French Governments respectively, remained as Subsonic Cruiser operators and, today, we each operate seven aircraft."

"So, where are we now, then, with the Cruiser?" Sir John enquired.

"We have established reasonably successful services on the routes from Heathrow to New York and Washington. However, flying by Cruiser only takes an hour or so off the journey. In comparison, the SST would have halved the travel time. We can charge premium fares for the Cruiser, but nothing like the levels of fares which would have been feasible with the SST."

"And what about the economics, Reggie?" Sir John further enquired.

"Not good. At the moment, we are operating the Cruiser fleet at around break-even, but future years will be different. We are currently paying a concessionary annual fleet rental of £5 million, as provided for in the Fleet Leasing & Purchase Agreement, which was signed by your predecessor in 1982. Interestingly, it was Lord Avonmouth who signed the Agreement on behalf of the Government. He was the Minister for Aerospace at the time. From the beginning of next year, the Agreement effectively obliges us to buy the aircraft fleet, spare engines and parts inventory, at an agreed price of £200 million payable over ten years."

"Pardon me, but my simple mind tells me that this change means we will save the £5 million annual rental but we will then incur a yearly capital cost of £20 million. So our annual costs will therefore increase effectively by a net £15 million. The operation presumably will then be significantly loss-making?"

"Unfortunately, you are absolutely correct, Chairman."

"Is there any get out?" Sir John enquired.

"Well, there is a clause in the Agreement which says that British International can elect not to proceed with the fleet purchase, if it can demonstrate that the operation of the aircraft is uneconomic. Given the huge expense to the Public purse in developing first the SST and then the Subsonic Cruiser and the national prestige associated with these projects, I suggest that to seek to exercise this get-out clause would be a most extreme course of action."

Sir John remained silent.

Lawrence said, "Thank you for that update, Reggie. Clearly, we need to task the Operations team to establish if there is any viable future plan for the Subsonic Cruiser operation, which we can present to the Department early next year."

By this stage, the trio was exhausted after a very full day. It was agreed that all key flotation issues had been discussed and that Lawrence and Reggie would now work on and would finalise the presentation to be made to the Department of Trade and Industry at the early January 1988 meeting.

Sir John commented that he would be giving some more thought to the Anglo-Scottish and Subsonic Cruiser issues with the benefit of the latest information, which had been provided during the meeting by Lawrence and Reggie.

Sir John then had to return urgently to Belgravia, where, instead of enjoying a peaceful evening, he was required to support Eleanor in hosting yet another social occasion. These events were now even more frequent. Eleanor was seizing every opportunity to show off the apartment's redecorations as orchestrated by Mr Desmond Pollock, together with the splendid furnishings which he had sourced and purchased, mostly regardless of cost.

Chapter 17
Cards on the Table

Lord Avonmouth, the former Michael Haughton MP, was now in his early fifties. He was an impressive figure, tall and lean with strong features and with a mane of swept back, now slightly greying, fair hair. From a middle-class background, he had been Public School-educated. Then, going up to Oxford, where he had engaged in University politics. His future political ambitions had been demonstrated by his successful election as President of the Oxford Union in recognition of his campaigning and managerial skills.

Upon leaving Oxford, with a degree in Politics, Philosophy and Economics, the classic degree for prospective politicians, he had used a small legacy to commence a London-based property development business. The business had been extremely successful both in buying properties for renovation and sale and also in building up a very large property rental portfolio. This portfolio had later been converted into a substantial Real Estate Investment Trust (REIT), which was now of a size that made it suitable for investment by pension schemes.

Haughton, always a strong supporter of the Conservative Party, had successfully contested a Bristol Parliamentary seat in the 1966 General Election. Having installed an experienced team at the REIT, whilst remaining as its Executive Chairman, he was now a wealthy man, well able to dedicate most of his time towards creating a Parliamentary career. He saw no reason at all why he should not reach the top of the political tree in relatively short order.

The British Aircraft Corporation facility and the adjacent Bristol Siddeley aero-engine factory at Filton, Bristol, were both within Haughton's constituency. So he had taken a close interest in the SST and, later, in the replacement Subsonic Cruiser project. Both plants were heavily Unionised, and Haughton was aware that, as the local Conservative MP, he was walking a difficult tightrope. When appointed Minister for Aerospace in the mid-1970s, he had been able to take a much more active role in the Subsonic Cruiser project. He had developed a strong personal interest in the aircraft, which he correctly regarded as being an outstanding British technical achievement. He had flown on the aircraft quite frequently, supporting a number of sales missions; all of which, sadly, had been unsuccessful. A consolation was that at least the Country's own major airline, the now British International Airlines, appeared to be successfully operating the type.

The Subsonic Cruiser operations were providing a steady stream of income, which was critical in sustaining employment at the Filton sites. Meanwhile, the Government was working hard to rebuild relations with Airbus, which was promising to place much-needed contract work at Bristol on its new A320 airliner. This desperately sought-after work should maintain and hopefully expand employment levels at Filton into the future.

His elevation to the peerage, as Lord Avonmouth, had been relatively recent, and he had been able to retain his current role as the President of the Board of Trade. He had certainly not given up on his ambitions to be Prime Minister. He had not been directly involved in the appointment of Sir John Cresswell as the Chairman of British International, who had been recommended by the Prime Minister for his initial term. He had never met the man, but he was aware of his reputation as being a bit of a rough diamond with a ruthless streak. So far as his lordship was concerned, he really did not care who was in charge at British International, so long as the individual delivered. If the Corporation was successfully privatised, his Department should then be accorded the appropriate kudos for having revived a sleeping giant and turned it into an internationally competitive world-beater. That would be an excellent result for both the Department and for him personally.

The day of the critical January 1988 joint pre-flotation meeting had now arrived. It was the first meeting at which the two headmen would be present. Lord Avonmouth was aware of a number of outstanding matters, as had been reported to him by his Departmental team. He would first need to raise the issue of Anglo-Scottish Airways, where its Chairman, Sir Adrian McClean, had been extremely persistent in pursuing his various demands. The Department had gained some respite recently by commissioning a Report from the Civil Aviation Authority on future route allocations. He now had the Report on his desk at his palatial office in Whitehall's Old Admiralty building. The Report had broadly concurred with the Anglo-Scottish proposals, a conclusion which was certainly not going to go down well with Sir John and his British International team.

Sir John, Lawrence, and Reggie, having navigated their way through the building's elaborate security procedures, were shown to a large conference table in Lord Avonmouth's office. His lordship had ensured that he was guarded by the Permanent Secretary and by a number of other senior Civil Servants, who were already assembled on the other side of the table.

"A very warm welcome to you, Sir John, and to your colleagues. We have met again at last, and I hope we can continue the excellent progress which our respective teams have been making."

Sir John responded. "Your lordship, thank you, I entirely concur. May I introduce our Chief Executive Officer, Lawrence Marshfield, who joined us two years ago and has since made a very positive impact. Also, our Company Secretary, Reginald Laycock, who has been with us man and boy. He knows all of the background. Are you happy for Lawrence to take the lead?"

"By all means, Sir John, please proceed, Mr Marshfield."

Lawrence took to the floor and circulated a short information pack containing the latest flotation financial analysis. He had previously enquired if the Department could make available a Personal Computer which would have enabled him to project the figures onto a screen. No reply had been forthcoming to that request.

"I believe that the figures indicate that a basis for a successful flotation can be achieved. However, I have made assumptions on certain issues which we now need to discuss and hopefully agree on."

"Of course, please carry on, Mr Marshfield." Responded Lord Avonmouth.

"As you know, the company has been significantly over-manned. We consider that, since this situation has occurred whilst the Airline has been in State ownership, the Government should be directly responsible for fifty percent of the redundancy costs involved in reducing manning to competitive levels. An associated issue is that of pensions. Mr Laycock has been doing a lot of work in this area, and the proposal is to close the Final Salary Pension Scheme when the flotation takes place and to replace it with a Money Purchase alternative. There is a funding deficit of around £250 million in the Final Salary Pension Scheme, and we believe that the Government should commit to putting this Scheme into balance at the point of flotation."

"Thank you, Mr Marshfield. You will appreciate that these are rather large asks. Any financial decisions will, of course, have to be made by the Treasury. However, we will certainly send your financial analysis and funding proposals to them for review. Just before you continue, there is one matter which I would like to mention at this stage."

Sir John, Lawrence, and Reggie steeled themselves as Lord Avonmouth continued.

"You will be aware of the long-standing Government policy to support and maintain a Second Force Private Sector airline. Anglo-Scottish Airways has very successfully performed this role for the last fifteen years or so, but as you know, current market conditions are very challenging. I have had a number of conversations with Sir Adrian McClean over the past year or so. Sir Adrian has made proposals to me which would entail the transfer of the British International Gatwick operations to Anglo-Scottish, together with a number of other British International routes. Sir Adrian tells me that Anglo-Scottish will soon be receiving its new Airbus A320s, so it will then be able to reorganise its aircraft fleet in order to service both its existing and these additional routes."

"I have asked the Civil Aviation Authority to report on Sir Adrian's proposals, and I have just received its Report. I must tell you that the Report appears to be broadly supportive. I should also mention that Sir Adrian has requested the Department to sponsor an amendment to the London Air Traffic Distribution Rules in order that Anglo-Scottish may operate some of its services from Heathrow. Do you have any comments on these proposals?"

Lawrence and Reggie stayed quiet. The floor now definitely belonged to Sir John to respond.

"Thank you for being so open, your lordship, and it will certainly be useful to see the CAA Report as soon as possible. You mention a "long-standing Government policy" concerning the Second Force Private Sector airline. I think a more accurate description would be a "long-outdated Government policy". The situation in the 1970s was very different from today, and I believe that Anglo-Scottish Airways has now served its purpose. The very reason that we are here this morning is to convert a State-owned airline corporation into a new, strong private-sector airline. What Sir Adrian is proposing would seriously undermine the proposed flotation, and it would make a complete nonsense of the figures which Mr Marshfield has just presented to you and your colleagues."

The Civil Service heads on the other side of the table were now nodding less vigorously, and Lord Avonmouth was looking decidedly uncomfortable. But Sir John had more to add.

"I have to say, your lordship, that Sir Adrian's proposals amount to nothing more than a 'smash and grab raid. I am absolutely sure that my Board will not countenance them or anything like them. If any operations or routes are taken away from British International Airlines, I will resign as Chairman. I am confident that my Board will follow suit.

It is composed of people whom I have personally recommended and who have joined the Airline on the basis that the flotation will be pursued by optimising our operations, not by butchering them!"

Lord Avonmouth was now even more unhappy, and his face was reddening with growing anger.

"Sir John, I really think that your response is most extreme and rather ill-considered."

"Lord Avonmouth, on the contrary. I have been broadly aware of Sir Adrian's proposals for some time. I can assure you that we have fully reviewed them and that my response is made after having taken due consideration of the likely consequences of their adoption. I am afraid there is nothing further I can usefully add, other than to express the opinion that a far more sensible course of action would be for British International to acquire Anglo-Scottish. An amalgamation of the two airlines would create a very strong independent British force in international civil aviation."

An uncomfortable silence followed. Lawrence and Reggie exchanged glances; the Chairman had never previously mentioned resigning. Also, the Board currently knew very little about the Anglo-Scottish situation, other than that the Airline was experiencing some turbulence. This new idea of possibly acquiring Anglo-Scottish was entirely of Sir John's invention. It had certainly never been presented to the Board, let alone had any such proposal been agreed by it! Perhaps the Chairman had cast his mind back to the mid-1960s when British Empire Airways had taken control, for a short period, of Sir Adrian's predecessor company. British Empire Airways had then proceeded to denude McClean's Scott-Air of its potentially competing routes, and Sir Adrian had felt obliged to buy back what remained of the depleted company.

Lawrence decided to break the silence. "Is it in order for me to proceed to the next item?"

Lord Avonmouth was mulling over the interesting prospect which had just been raised by Sir John. A takeover of Anglo-Scottish was a possibility that had apparently escaped the minds of the gathered Civil Servants, a good number of whom in the Department were supposed experts in the civil aviation sector.

"Apologies, Mr Marshfield, please continue, and hopefully we will now find some common ground."

Lawrence thought to himself, "Unfortunately, I very much doubt that."

"There is only really one remaining major topic, which is fleet replacement and economics. The good news is that our twin Rolls-Royce RB211-powered Boeing 757s are now arriving. By early next year, we will have completed the introduction of these new aircraft and will have phased out all of our time-expired Tridents on our medium-haul operations. In the long-haul fleet, we are replacing our early Jumbo jets with the latest, Rolls-Royce RB211-powered versions. We will continue to make good use of our fleet of Lockheed Tristars, which are also RB211-powered, until they are retired in the mid-1990s."

"That is excellent news." Purred Lord Avonmouth.

Lawrence continued, "The situation is not so bright in the short-haul business. The One Eleven twinjets have served us well, but they are thirsty and noisy, and new regulations will prohibit their operation after 1990. We are increasing our fleet of Boeing 737s, but they are not as efficient as the Airbus A320. We need prompt Government authorisation to place an order for this new Airbus aircraft as soon as possible."

"I hear what you say, Mr Marshfield, concerning the need for A320s, and I can assure you that I will be discussing this issue with my colleagues. Now, is there anything else?"

"Just the matter of the Subsonic Cruiser."

"Really," said Lord Avonmouth. "A very fine aircraft and a tribute both to British and French engineering and to the excellent collaboration between the two countries. You may know that I have had a long personal involvement in the project. It is a great shame that external pressures enforced changes to the original specification."

Lawrence resumed, the next few minutes were going to be very tricky.

"I am aware of your previous close involvement, your lordship, and I believe that you were once a Bristol MP. As you say, the Subsonic Cruiser is a fine aircraft, but due to the specification changes to which you have referred, the travel time advantages that it offers over the Jumbo are much less than would have been the case with the originally conceived Supersonic Transport. We can charge slightly higher fares, but the Cruiser's seat/mile costs are three times greater than those of the Jumbo. Also, the Cruiser will soon be the only aircraft in our fleet that requires a Flight Engineer in addition to the two pilots."

"I am not sure what you are trying to tell me, Mr Marshfield."

"What I am leading to, your lordship, is that our Operations Team has concluded that the continued operation of the Subsonic Cruiser fleet by British International is uneconomic for the Airline. To continue Supersonic Cruiser services would be a major negative for the proposed flotation."

Lord Avonmouth was becoming tense and uncomfortable and growing even redder in the face.

"I find what you have just said, Mr Marshfield, to be quite impossible to accept. Surely there are many ways in which a profitable operation could be established?"

At this point, Sir John decided to intervene.

"Your lordship, my colleagues and I have been wrestling with this issue for some time. The 1982 Lease and Purchase Agreement, which I believe you signed when you were Minister of Aerospace, provides for the leasing of the Cruiser fleet for an initial five years at a rental of £5 million per annum. Thereafter, British International may purchase the fleet and its associated spare engines and parts inventory for the amount of £200 million payable over ten years."

"Yes, Sir John, I recollect the Agreement very clearly. The initial leasing terms were very favourable to the Airline, and it is equally clear that British International is obligated to purchase the fleet next year and that it has a responsibility to make Cruiser operations more viable. I should mention also that the £200 million purchase price was an absolute bargain, being less than ten percent of the Cruiser's development and construction costs."

"Your lordship, I think it might be helpful at this point if I asked our Company Secretary to say a few words. I believe he has the 1982 Agreement with him."

Reggie was not expecting Sir John's invitation to contribute, but, fortunately, he had the Agreement sitting in front of him, amongst his other papers, which were piled on the table.

"I can confirm to your lordship that the financial terms are as stated by Sir John. If British International was to purchase the fleet, then any such transaction would need to take place before the target date for flotation."

"Mr Laycock, you have just used the word 'if'. I am now very unclear."

"Your lordship, I used the word 'if' because of Clause 25 in the Agreement."

"Kindly remind me, Mr Laycock, of what this Clause contains," said his lordship, glaring down the table at the massed ranks of Civil Servants.

"In a nutshell, the Clause provides that British International is not obligated to purchase the Subsonic Cruiser fleet if it deems that it is uneconomic to continue the operation of the aircraft."

Sir John now made a further intervention.

"Your lordship will, no doubt, have already calculated that the economic impact on British International of purchasing and continuing to operate the Subsonic Cruiser fleet will be to replace the annual rental of £5 million with an annual purchase instalment cost of £20 million. A net cost increase to the business of £15 million per annum. There can therefore be no doubt that the Cruiser operation will then be totally uneconomic. Its continuation will potentially jeopardise the proposed flotation of British International, unless the Government is prepared to underwrite the losses."

The anger within Lord Avonmouth was rising further.

"Do you have a proposal to make, Sir John?"

"Yes indeed, your lordship, the British International Board has discussed this matter and has concluded that Subsonic Cruiser operations can only be continued if the fleet, including spare engines and the parts inventory, is acquired by British International for a single payment of £20 million."

There was an almost audible gasp around the table as Sir John delivered his second proposal of the morning. Lawrence and Reggie exchanged quick glances again. To their knowledge, there had never been any discussion around the Board table concerning the future of the Subsonic Cruiser fleet and its operations!

"Sir John, once again, I believe you are adopting a most extreme and unhelpful position. We signed an Agreement in 1982, and I expect British International to adhere to the spirit of that Agreement."

"Your lordship, the Agreement makes it quite clear that British International is not obligated to purchase the aircraft fleet for £200 million. If you do not accept our revised offer, then Subsonic Cruiser operations will cease at the end of March. The fleet will then be returned to Filton. We believe that the proposed £20 million is a fair price. You cannot expect British International to be responsible for the follies of the past."

There was a stunned silence. The last remark had really stung. A now incandescent Lord Avonmouth effectively shouted across the table.

"I will not have a gun held to my head. I am one of Her Majesty's Ministers, and I will not be threatened in this manner. The return of the Subsonic Cruiser fleet to Filton would amount to nothing less than a national humiliation."

Lawrence and Reggie had similar thoughts. Yes, not only a national humiliation, but it would be a personal humiliation for his lordship and one which would almost certainly spell the end of his political career.

Having recovered some of his composure, Lord Avonmouth rapidly drew the meeting to a close, stating that they could not proceed any further in the meantime, because there was so much follow-up work to do. Many meetings would be needed between the respective teams over the next few months to resolve the final issues in the lead-up to the proposed flotation in May.

The trio from British International was escorted from the building and out onto the Mall, where Gerry was waiting with the BMW 7 Series. Sir John had finally lost patience with Rolls-Royce Motors. He had punished them by persuading British International to go German and to acquire the BMW as a replacement for the Silver Spirit.

"Well, that was a bit of fun, wasn't it?" said Sir John. Most enjoyable to see his lordship teetering on the brink, perhaps I should have given him one final push! I suggest a spot of lunch is now well merited. "I hope you gentlemen will join me at Whites."

Lawrence and Reggie readily agreed, a little relaxation was called for after such a highly stressful morning.

"I am looking forward, Lawrence, to hearing how you and that beautiful wife of yours are settling in at Weybridge. I am sure that Reggie will entertain us over lunch with his latest jokes. I only wish I knew where he finds them."

Chapter 18
Moving On and an Invitation

When the Hansard Group takeover announcement of the Mid-lands & West Group had been made back in late October 1987, it was obvious to all at Corporate Office that it would be terminal for every-one employed there. For some of the bright young things, the takeover presented an early opportunity to collect a redundancy payment and to move on, hopefully, to better things. Exhausted by his nearly three years of ultimately unsuccessful troubleshooting travel, Mike Holland was one of the first to jump ship in order to join a start-up company engaged in manufacturing airships.

The £50 million paid into the M&G Group Final Salary Pension Scheme would facilitate early retirement packages for those who qual-ified by virtue of being within five years of retirement and also having worked with the Group for more than ten years. This was a benefit improvement upon which Sir John had personally insisted. Both Jen-nifer Palmer and Harry Shining were in the qualifying group. All for-mer Corporate Office employees would receive redundancy payments, but those needing to remain in employment would now have to fend for themselves in a competitive job market.

By early 1988, the King Street office was emptying rapidly. Miss Palmer and Harry Shining had agreed to stay on until the final closure date, which would be the 31 March. Sir John remained in situ for the meantime and was negotiating with Lawrence for the establishment of a Central London Chairman's Office for British International Airlines. Lawrence had acted tough, finally agreeing only to the provision of a small serviced office in a swish new block in nearby Buckingham Gate. Sir John had asked Miss Palmer if she would continue to work for him part-time. Miss Palmer had politely declined. Sir John would now have to be at the mercy of the typing services, which were included within the serviced office package. After all her years of training, she was reasonably confident, however, that the standard of Sir John's letters would be passable, even without her ongoing supervision and editing.

Lawrence Marshfield had continued his regular visits to King Street for his Monday meetings with the Chairman. Miss Palmer had now typed a large volume of letters for him, as had become the established practice, and so Lawrence's correspondence was completely up to date. She had noticed, however, that the need for her subtle adjustments to Mr Marshfield's letters had become much less necessary.

In late March, there had been an unexpected invitation. Mr Marshfield had insisted that Miss Palmer should join him for a farewell lunch. Gerry, who was to be the only survivor of the Midlands & West Group corporate staff, had been added to the chauffeurs' pool at British International. He was now waiting in King Street below with the BMW 7 Series.

The somewhat unusual venue for the lunch was the cafeteria at the top of the John Lewis store on Oxford Street. Miss Palmer didn't mind at all; she was a regular customer of the store. It was here that she purchased her modest office suits, with their below-the-knee length, pleated skirts. However, never had she arrived in such chauffeured style. It was all rather thrilling. Over a pleasant light lunch, Mr Marshfield had done most of the talking. He related the story of how he had met his beautiful wife, Lisa, when they were both at Oceanic Transport & Trading, and he had shown Miss Palmer some recent photos of his wife and children. It was clear that he was still deeply in love with Lisa. Miss Palmer had been a bit of a dancer in her youth, but she had not been so fortunate. Some people have all the luck, she mused. However, I am enjoying today and, with retirement now imminent, I am excited to be about to embark upon a new phase of my life.

On the way down from the cafeteria, Lawrence had diverted from the route to the front entrance. If there was to be any such detour, then Miss Palmer would have favoured a visit to the Sports Department in order to inspect the latest line of Lawn Bowls footwear. As it was, she found herself scuttling after Lawrence and following him into the Electricals Department. Her luncheon companion was heading in the direction of the Personal Computers.

"Now, Miss Palmer, which one would you prefer?"

"Well, actually, none of them, Mr Marshfield. I am very happy with my Selectric and I share Sir John's opinion that these things are just a passing trend, which will definitely not catch on."

"You are correct, Miss Palmer, that I have failed to convince Sir John. However, I promise you that by the end of this week, you will be converted. Now, please make a choice. This is a gift to you from me personally and from British International for your much-appreciated help and contribution."

Miss Palmer reluctantly pointed to the grey box, which she considered to be the least offensive.

"An excellent choice, if I may say Miss Palmer. Kevin from our IT Department will make the collection tomorrow and will then come to the office for your first tutorial."

"Mr Marshfield, I really think that I am a little too old to be learning new tricks. I am most grateful for your consideration, but I cannot see that I will have any possible future use for this device, which, if I heard you correctly, is called a Personal Computer?"

"Yes, Miss Palmer, exactly, it is indeed a Personal Computer, and it is the future. You must appreciate that without the lifeline of full-time employment, you could soon become rather lonely and isolated at home. My parents have recently retired to the Wirral. My mother has always been keen on new technology, and so I bought them a Personal Computer as a retirement present. Even my father, who can be a bit of a Luddite at times, has found that it is an excellent way of keeping in touch and also for organising paperwork."

Lawrence continued, "Computers will soon be able to talk to each other across the world. I am pretty sure that the next step will be to enable people to pay their bills and to order groceries by using them. I suggest that a Personal Computer will be an important friend to you as you age gracefully in retirement. My colleague, Kevin, will be along in the morning, and I am confident that you will find exploring computing with him to be a most rewarding experience."

Chapter 19
The Tutorial Student

The following morning, Miss Palmer waited anxiously in her office. The message had just reached her from the downstairs Reception that her visitor had arrived and that he was making his way to the first floor. Miss Palmer was not expecting to be impressed, and she was duly vindicated. The huffing and puffing, rucksack-carrying Kevin was clad in jeans and a pullover. In his arms was a large carton which, Miss Palmer assumed contained the hideous item purchased yesterday. Miss Palmer also thought that the bespectacled Kevin could do with a jolly good haircut and shave. However, she must not judge simply by appearances, however tempting that may be.

"Hi Ya", greeted Kevin as he plonked the rucksack and the heavy carton on Miss Palmer's side table, which she normally used for collating and filing.

"And a good morning to you also. Am I correct that your Christian name is Kevin?"

"Yeah, that's me." Kevin was busy extracting the previously-selected Personal Computer, together with its monitor and keyboard, from the carton, and he was just about to carry the items over to Miss Palmer's desk.

"No, no, please leave those things exactly where they are. There is an electrical point behind the side table, and I will come over to you."

"OK," said Kevin, "I will plug in and away we will go."

The computer whirred. Kevin pressed a few keys and the monitor burst into colourful life.

"Now, Miss Palmer, please would you be so kind as to type in this paragraph?"

Kevin produced a dog-eared typed piece of paper, and Miss Palmer sat down at the table. She was pleased to see a QWERTY keyboard in front of her, and she was beginning to feel a little bit more at ease. It was uncomfortable and rather strange, however, not to insert a piece of paper into the machine. Miss Palmer flexed her fingers and rapidly demolished the typing exercise, without once looking at the keyboard.

"Wow, that was most impressive! Part of the exercise is to demonstrate how to correct errors, but you haven't made any. No matter, let's pretend you have missed out a word."

"I never miss out words."

"I fully understand that, Miss Palmer, but let us just pretend for once that you did. So let's type the words "personal computer" here into line two."

Miss Palmer thought Kevin might have chosen these words just to annoy her.

"I assume that each word should start with a capital letter?"

Kevin looked blank and uncomfortable. He avoided making a reply by focusing his attention on manipulating the keyboard.

"Now, Miss Palmer, please type in the words, which I suggested, in whatever form you think to be appropriate."

Miss Palmer typed in the words "Personal Computer," which magically appeared in line two. Miss Palmer was now becoming much more interested. She could not count how many times in the past she had had to retype letters completely when it had been necessary to make last-minute changes. Could this machine potentially eliminate all of that wasted time and paper?

The session continued for an hour, during which time Kevin demonstrated the many other ways in which documents could be edited and formatted. Miss Palmer was rapidly becoming a fan.

"I think that is enough for us today, Miss Palmer, and so I will see you tomorrow."

"What do you mean by tomorrow? I hope you are not going to leave those things with me."

"I most certainly am. My instructions from that CEO guy, Mr Marshfield, are for me to carry on our sessions for the next two days. Here are some exercises for you to practice, so that we can have a running start tomorrow. I will also bring along and install the printer, which is part of the package. It was too much for me to carry today. I will then show you how to print items. Later in the week, we will move on to the setting up and use of spreadsheets."

Kevin picked up his rucksack, and he had left the office before Miss Palmer could protest.

Miss Palmer returned to her desk. She sat down and eyed the Personal Computer and its associated ancillary items lurking on the side table. "I will leave you alone for a few hours. But, funny grey box that you are, you don't frighten me any more. So let's meet again later this afternoon."

Chapter 20
Farewell to King Street

There was no computer training session on Friday, because this was now the 31 March 1988, and it was the last day of operations for the former Midlands & West Group Corporate office. Harry Shining had been instructed to arrange a farewell party, and he had much enjoyed making some pretty unreasonable demands on the prima-donna cook, who had been retained for this one last occasion in order to provide a top-quality buffet lunch. Harry was content that, this time, he could allow her to leave the kitchen in her usual chaotic state. The lease on the office expired at the end of the month, and so a deep clean of the entire floor would be necessary as part of the process of handing back to the landlord.

Miss Palmer had completed her lessons with Kevin the previous day. Gerry had then helped her to clear her office, and the Personal Computer, monitor, keyboard, and printer had taken pride of place as she was chauffeured home to Barking. Also on board was the Selectric, which the company had gifted to her, but she had a funny feeling that she would not be finding much future use for it.

Sir John was alone in his corner office for the final time. Outside was a dismal winter's day with St James's Square looking equally out of sorts. Nature had little activity to offer in order to alleviate the external gloom. He was pensively sitting at the conference table. The maroon leather-surfaced desk had been another casualty of the office closure. It would not fit into the cellular glass-partitioned office at Hounslow. The serviced office in Buckingham Gate, which he had eventually reluctantly agreed to occupy, was fully furnished. Also, the Belgravia apartment was now restored and was stocked full of expensive furniture, following the ministrations of Desmond Pollock. Eleanor had made it quite clear that the desk was welcome neither there nor back at Bishop's Lake.

Fortunately, Andrew claimed to have contacts in the antiques trade. So the maroon desk, together with the cut glass ink wells, silver tray, and silver coated writing implements, had been handed over to a dealer.

Presumably, a new home would be found. It would be interesting to see if Andrew volunteered to produce the net sale proceeds.

It was a great shame to have been faced with no real option other than to allow the Midlands & West Group to disappear, and most frustrating that the upstart Hansard had had his evil way. Sir John addressed the framed photograph of Laura, which he was about to transfer into his briefcase.

"Well, my love, it seems that we have reached the end of a long saga. I know you will be disappointed that we have lost the Midlands & West Group, but I believe I have done my best for the employees. Now it is time for us to move ahead once again and to get on with our next adventure."

Sir John placed the photograph into his briefcase.

However, there was a silver lining, thought Sir John. Although he had lost the substantial salary he had hitherto commanded as Executive Chairman of the Midlands & West Group, he had succeeded in achieving a very smooth exit. The Cresswell Family Investment Company's five percent shareholding had been realised without any difficulty, albeit at a much lower price than that prevailing twelve months previously. The proceeds had been used to increase the Investment Company's other varied shareholdings.

British International was now financially responsible for the provision of the Belgravia apartment and was servicing his transportation needs with the new BMW. Sir John was also confident that directors' emoluments at British International would be reviewed, post the flotation, which should now not be too far away. Some of his lost Midlands & West Group salary would then be effectively replaced by a much higher Chairman's fee. British International would be a public company and, assuming he secured an extended term of office as Chairman, he would be able to enjoy ongoing market-rate emoluments until the end of May 1995.

This outcome would be an appropriate reward for his having revitalised and floated the company. The value of his shares in British International should progressively increase, and there would, doubtless, be further share allotments. Periodic subsequent share sales, as and when the prices were right, should supplement Sir John's income during those final pre-retirement years and would continue throughout his ensuing retirement.

Sir John entered the King Street main office, where there was a gathering of the remaining Corporate Office staff, together with some professional advisers; around forty attendees in total. Miss Palmer and Harry Shining were present, delighted that they would both benefit from the M&W Group Final Salary Pension Scheme early retirement plan. They would be receiving unreduced early retirement pensions, albeit that they would lose some pensionable service as a result of not being able to work through to their normal retirement dates.

Lady Eleanor, clad in Burberry in anticipation of her forthcoming weekend at Bishop's Lake, was never known to miss a good party. She was engaged in earnest conversation with Miss Palmer, who was extolling to her ladyship the virtues of modern computing. Miss Palmer was convinced that Personal Computers were definitely the future. Sir John overheard some of this exchange. He had a funny feeling that the large and unkempt figure, whom he had noted visiting Miss Palmer's office on several occasions earlier in the week, might soon be instructing another pupil!

Harry Shining was busy rushing around the room, ensuring that all present were well-fed and watered. He managed to catch Sir John's eye.

"Sir John, I think this may be the last opportunity for us to speak. I just wanted to thank you for allowing me to manage the Corporate Office and for ensuring that the pensions of the older Group employees have been protected. It means a lot to us."

"Not at all, Harry, I have enjoyed our banter over the years. So what are you going to do now?"

"Well, as you know, my wife and I are happily settled in Hove. My daughter and son-in-law run a local estate agency down there. I have offered my services to them for showing properties to prospective purchasers and renters. Strangely, their response, so far, has not been very positive, but I am very confident they will accept my assistance. However, I have also been having some interesting thoughts recently on new document handling equipment. There is an office equipment and systems business down the road, in Portslade, and I have already been to see them. They seemed to be very interested in my ideas, but that was a couple of weeks ago. They have not yet come back to me, but I am very confident that they will."

Sir John thought to himself, well, if they have any sense at all, they should definitely stay clear!

"Most interesting, Harry, good luck in all that you do, and I wish you and your dear wife good health and happiness in the future."

Sir John then made a speech recounting the milestones and key moments of the Midlands & West Group and ending with a couple of jokes which he had pinched from Reggie's extensive repertoire.

The party was at an end. Those present would now move on with their future lives. Sir John was optimistic about the future. If he was successful in achieving the flotation of British International Airlines, an extension to his current term of office as Chairman was surely guaranteed. Further, why would the Government not sponsor his final ascent into the heights of British Society by way of supporting a successful application for a peerage?

Chapter 21
Duplicity

Sir Adrian McClean considered that he had waited an excessively long time for his late January 1988 meeting with Lord Avonmouth. The Department had suspended discussions in the autumn of the previous year, pending the publication of the Civil Aviation Authority Report, which it had commissioned on the future allocation of air routes. But that Report had been published nearly three months ago and his understanding, through informal contacts, was that it was clearly supportive of the proposals that he had made to British International as far back as in May 1986.

Sir Adrian had long given up any prospect of any constructive follow-up with Sir John Cresswell, subsequent to that May 1986 meeting. Sir John had spent the last nearly two years fabricating a series of poor excuses. This kind of conduct was, regrettably, only to be expected from British International. Sir Adrian was still mindful of the British Empire Airways part-takeover of his original airline, Scott-Air, back in the mid-1960s. He had entered into that transaction in good faith, only to find that it was simply a cynical attempt by British Empire Airways to circumscribe the operations of Scott-Air and to remove a competitor.

He had hoped for better from the President of the Board of Trade, but at least the delay in today's meeting had enabled him to work up the Anglo-Scottish contingency plans with Scandavia and with Package Europe. It was even possible that all three entities might combine, which would create quite a formidable unit.

"Good morning, Sir Adrian", breezed Lord Avonmouth.

Here was a man who had clearly regained his mojo, following the bruising meeting with British International a few weeks previously. After that meeting, he had been called in to Downing Street to report the outcome to the Prime Minister. They had discussed both the Anglo-Scottish situation and the Subsonic Cruiser fleet. With regard to the latter issue, Lord Avonmouth had stated that he believed the Government had unfortunately been placed in a position where it had no cards to play. The Prime Minister had reluctantly agreed. The Subsonic Cruiser fleet would be sold to British International in March 1988 for the "bargain basement" price offered by Sir John. However, neither politician had appreciated the indignity of being manoeuvred into this situation, and they would neither easily forget nor would they forgive.

"Now what can I do for you, Sir Adrian?"

"I am rather surprised that you ask that question, your lordship. I am simply here to receive your confirmation that the Department endorses what I understand to be the CAA Report's conclusions on route allocations. Anglo-Scottish can then pursue its negotiations with British International in order to acquire its Gatwick operations and also those additional routes of which the Department has been made aware. In addition, we are awaiting confirmation from the Department that actions will be taken to modify the London Air Traffic Distribution Rules, so that Anglo-Scottish can operate some services from Heathrow. These changes are essential in order to maintain the Government's long-standing policy for the maintenance of a strong Second Force Private Sector airline."

"Yes indeed Sir Adrian. I can assure you that my colleagues and I have been burning the midnight oil in order to establish the best way forward for British civil aviation. You correctly refer to a long-standing Government policy for the maintenance of a Second Force Private Sector airline. However, I believe it is true to say that this policy was conceived in the late 1960s when circumstances were very different."

Alarm bells started to ring in Sir Adrian's head.

Lord Avonmouth continued.

"The Government is now of the view that the proposed flotation of British International Airlines, hopefully later this year, fundamentally changes the situation. The Country will then have another strong Private Sector airline, and the Department has concluded that there is no rationale for supporting two Private Sector airlines."

"So you are stabbing us in the back, then." Exploded Sir Adrian.

"Not at all, Sir Adrian, and I am sorry that you are taking that view. We are simply saying that Anglo-Scottish will need to continue making its excellent progress under your inspired leadership and management, but without the Department effecting the changes which you have requested."

The news that Lord Avonmouth had just presented was not entirely unexpected, and so Sir Adrian decided to test out his contingency plans.

"Your lordship, as I have endeavoured to explain previously, I am afraid that, with the best will in the world, Anglo-Scottish cannot continue to operate for much longer as it is currently constituted. We will, of course, maintain our lobbying for the changes which I have previously requested. However, as you would expect, we have contingency plans, but I had very much hoped they would not be necessary. May I outline these plans to you now?"

"By all means, Sir Adrian, I would very much like to hear what might be possible."

"Your lordship will be aware of the successful Scandinavian Airline, Scandavia and also of the innovative airline, Package Europe, which has grown very quickly in recent years?"

"Yes, I know both airlines. Please continue."

"Each of these airlines is interested in making future arrangements with Anglo-Scottish. Scandavia is proposing to take a majority shareholding, whilst a transaction with Package Europe would involve Anglo-Scottish taking over that airline's operations. This second transaction would require quite a lot of highly leveraged finance. There is also an option of all three airlines combining. Do you or the Department have a view on any of these possibilities?"

"Sir Adrian, as you would expect, my colleagues are monitoring the state of the British civil aviation market on a continuous basis. What you have just said is not a complete surprise, so I am able to make some preliminary comments now which I trust will be helpful."

Lord Avonmouth continued.

"With regard to Scandavia, this is, of course, a foreign-owned airline. In order to keep its route licences, the Government will require Anglo-Scottish to continue to be owned by a majority of British-based shareholders. I regret to say, therefore, that the sale of a majority holding to Scandavia must be considered as a non-starter. Concerning Package Europe, this airline has been on the CAA watch list for some time. The CAA has determined that it has few, if any, owned assets. I would also say that its operations appear to have little or no compatibility with those of Anglo-Scottish."

"Package Europe is currently in breach of a number of its Operating Licences, and the CAA is seriously concerned that it will be unable to pay the deposit required shortly, in order to continue its membership of the ATOL scheme. As you well know, Sir Adrian, the ATOL scheme protects package holiday customers and ensures that they are flown home in the event of a failure of the holiday provider. Without membership of ATOL, it is difficult to see how Package Europe will be able to continue. I can understand why they have been talking to you. I believe they are just desperately seeking a lifeline."

Sir Adrian's contingency plans had just been effectively torpedoed.

"It seems to me that your lordship is adopting a rather entrenched position here. If what you say is correct, then Anglo-Scottish has nowhere to go. A failure of the Airline, I suggest, would be a matter of

National disquiet and consequence and would show the Government to be in a very poor light."

"On the contrary, Sir Adrian, I think that there is a very clear way forward with substantial benefits for all parties involved."

Lord Avonmouth withdrew a slim folder from his left-hand desk draw and passed it over the table to Sir Adrian.

"I will not beat about the bush, Sir Adrian. In our flotation discussions with British International, I have reached the conclusion that the best way for the Country to maintain a strong Private Sector Independent airline would be through a combination of British International and Anglo-Scottish. I was successful in persuading Sir John Cresswell and his Board that this proposal is the best option for everyone. The document which you have in your hands is an offer from British International to acquire Anglo-Scottish for the amount of £125 million. We have given the pricing our full consideration, we think it is very fair and it will not be increased."

"So you are presenting me with a fait accompli then?"

"I would not put it in quite those terms, Sir Adrian. You are receiving a very fair offer as a result of which you, personally, as the majority shareholder in Anglo-Scottish, will become a very rich man. In addition, you will see, in the document, a letter from Sir John, inviting you to join the British International Board as its Deputy Chairman. We think that such an appointment would be an appropriate recognition of your undisputed high status in the Industry."

Sir Adrian glanced at the letter and also in the direction of the waste bin at the corner of his lordship's desk. He thought, yes, you pompous man, this proposed takeover is nothing less than an ambush, and it was certainly not you who contrived this idea. You know what you and the invisible Sir John can do with that palliative piece of paper!

Sir Adrian departed from the Department shortly afterwards. So far as he was concerned, he had just been bullied out of his own company. It would be his last visit to that archaic Government building. As Lord Avonmouth had said, he was now about to become a rich man, although he would not be changing his modest lifestyle. Some consolation was that he had recently been invited to Chair the Institute of Directors for the next three years. He would at last be able to put the aviation world behind him; a change of scene was definitely what he very much needed.

Chapter 22
A Dramatic Year and a Knighthood

The autumn of 1988 had arrived, after what had already been the most dramatic year yet in the life of British International Airlines. It had been a transformational year and one of great progress. The Subsonic Cruiser fleet had not been returned to Filton in March, as Sir John had threatened. On the contrary, the Government's reluctant agreement to the £20 million fleet purchase price had eliminated the £5 million per annum rental charge and had enabled Subsonic operations to be put onto a more sustainable basis. The capital payment for the fleet and for the associated spare engines and parts inventory had been lost within the myriad of pre-flotation transactions effected between the Airline and the Government.

The Government had accepted its share of the British International redundancy costs, and the Final Salary Pension Scheme had been brought into balance, when it had been closed to new members and to future accrual at the point of flotation. The Airline was now on its own, concerning future redundancy plans and pensions arrangements.

The acquisition of Anglo-Scottish Airways had been completed on 30 April. The Anglo-Scottish head office at Horley had been closed immediately. Sir John had thought it strange that Sir Adrian McClean had declined his invitation to join the British International Board, but that was his choice. The integration of the Anglo-Scottish operations had been very quick. The leases were early-terminated on the ageing One Elevens and the now-arriving Airbus A320s were gratefully received for operation by British International from Heathrow. Since it now qualified as an existing A320 operator, British International had been able to place an order, at a much higher level in the queue, for a further fifteen aircraft. British International had transferred some of its Boeing 737s to Gatwick to operate the short and medium-haul Anglo-Scottish services formerly serviced by the time-expired One-Elevens. Most of the Anglo-Scottish long-haul aircraft were sold, with just a few of the newer aircraft being retained to fill gaps in the British International fleet.

Another airline sector event, which also occurred on 30 April 1988, was the announcement of the appointment of a Liquidator at Package Europe. The grapevine had once again correctly predicted the future train of events. Package Europe, with minimal owned assets and having incurred large finance and leasing costs, had finally run out of road. The bankers had withdrawn their support, once it had become clear that there was no possibility of any kind of a deal with Anglo-Scottish. There were no funds available to continue Package Europe's membership of the ATOL scheme, and so the airline had ceased operations.

A tidied-up and much more efficient British International Airlines had more than met the expectations of the City of London. The Government had appointed the "blue chip" merchant bankers, Cavendish & Co, to launch the flotation. The bankers had done an excellent job. Support had been forthcoming from the major Institutional Investors, which had enabled the shares issue to be fully underwritten. The Government had insisted that the majority of the shares should be offered to the General Public, and the offer had taken place as scheduled on 31 May 1988. Such was the interest that no underwriting was necessary, and the offer was over-subscribed six times. The Government would retain a "Golden share" for a five-year period, which was designed to stop any takeover occurring during that time. The Government would also retain the right to appoint the new company's Chairman for so long as it held the Golden share.

An event had occurred during July 1988, which had been celebrated widely within British International and particularly in Staines, Tranmere and in New York. The Queen's Birthday Honours List had included the name of Lawrence Marshfield. The British International Chief Executive Officer, still only in his mid-forties, had been awarded a knighthood.

Sir John was delighted to see Lawrence being honoured in this fashion, but he could not entirely hide his disappointment that, at least for the meantime, his personal hopes for elevation to the peerage had been dashed. There had been no intimation from the Government of its support for an application for him to join the House of Lords. It seemed to Sir John that he would have to make just one more last push. Some kind of initiative was needed, to which he could put his name, and which would take British International to new heights. His smooth progression into the peerage then surely should just be a formality.

Lisa accompanied her husband to the October investiture ceremony at Windsor Castle, looking fabulous in her formal outfit. Later in the month, the couple had left the children with Lisa's parents, over half term, in order to visit the Wirral, where Lawrence's father was in the last few weeks of his life. Two years previously, Lawrence had overseen the sale of the Tranmere sub-post office and the tobacconist and sweets business. He had then ensured the safe installation of his parents into assisted living accommodation, together with the Personal Computer which he had purchased for them. The pleasant development which they had chosen overlooked the Mersey estuary. Here, Ted Marshfield had been able to spend his declining years, enthusiastically observing the marine traffic progressing into and out of the Port.

During their visit, Lawrence and Lisa, or more correctly now, Sir Lawrence and Lady Marshfield, had also fulfilled an invitation to be Guests of Honour at the Speech Day and Prize-giving at Lawrence's old school. The pupils and staff were fascinated to see and to hear the man, who was now both a Knight of the Realm and was also the Chief

Executive Officer of one of Britain's largest and most high-profile companies. He was, by a considerable margin, the school's most successful and famous former pupil.

Old classmates had also sent their congratulations. Not least Geoff Prescott, who had invited Lawrence to speak to most of the country's leading Rugby Union players, who were attending his Club's Annual Dinner. Geoff had suggested, tongue in cheek, that the subject should be how the uncannily accurate positional play of a school Second XV full back had later enabled him to scale the heights of British Industry! There was even a short congratulatory note from Miss Palmer. Lawrence had ensured that his reply to Miss Palmer had incorporated his very best attempts at writer's flair.

Back at Hounslow in the autumn of 1988, Sir John was now visiting the Headquarters more often for his regular updates with Lawrence. First usually calling by Reggie's office for their little chats, and in order for Sir John to absorb Reggie's latest jokes.

The two had then joined Lawrence in his office. Despite the outstanding successes achieved so far this year, Sir John was still niggled by one issue which he considered had not yet been adequately addressed.

"Sir Lawrence, or is it in order if I still just call you Lawrence?" Joked Sir John.

"Lawrence is a perfectly adequate form of address. So long as I can continue to call you Chairman." Replied Lawrence in a similar vein.

"It seems that something is still bothering you. What is it?"

"It's this wretched Atlantic Fortress Airways situation. You will recollect that I raised it with you soon after you joined us. You assured me that it was not a concern, but I see that they are now operating five Jumbos and have added Miami and Orlando to their schedules. I believe Atlantic Fortress is becoming a threat and that we should be jolly well doing something about it."

"Sir John, my experience of working with you, for nearly three years now, is that you have invariably thought through these situations and already have proposals to make. What are they?"

"Well, it seems to me that part of the reason for Atlantic Fortress's success is that they are undercutting our fares. Surely if we had a few quiet words with our other, much longer-established, competitors on the transatlantic routes, then we might come to a short-term arrangement, collectively to reduce our own fares. We could then squeeze Atlantic Fortress out of the market. Once we have got rid of them, we could progressively restore fares to sensible levels."

Lawrence frowned and responded.

"Sir John, that is no doubt an excellent commercial idea; however, it would also be a flagrant breach of Competition Law! We currently have a £50 million Provision in the Accounts relating to the Laker Skytrain affair back in 1982. Obviously, neither of us was involved at the time, but the then management was accused of almost exactly what you have just suggested. Freddie Laker called it a conspiracy and set about suing all and sundry, including British International. The legal case is still outstanding, but our advice is that it should be settled. Now that we are a publicly quoted company, we cannot have litigation hanging over us. I expect we will pay out the Provision later this year when the settlement takes place."

"Really, Lawrence, are you quite sure that you are not being excessively bureaucratic and cautious?"

"Absolutely sure, Chairman. If we were caught up in another alleged conspiracy to fix fares, then the consequences would be very serious indeed. Do you have any further suggestions?"

"Well, actually, I do have one other. How do we sell our tickets?"

"Currently mostly through Travel Agents, with the remainder being sold by direct telephone bookings."

"Surely we can initiate some kind of arrangement to incentivise Travel Agents to favour the sales of British International tickets. For example, if a Travel Agent is currently selling British International and Atlantic Fortress tickets in the ratio 60:40, could we not encourage them to improve the ratio to, say, 90:10 by awarding them some kind of rebate?"

"You mean something like a fidelity rebate," commented Lawrence.

"Yes, that is exactly what I have in mind, if that's how you would describe it. I think this kind of incentive payment would be a most excellent arrangement, and it seems perfectly uncontentious to me."

"A fidelity rebate is precisely how I would describe it, and, regrettably, Chairman, the implementation of any such arrangement would be highly contentious. A few years ago, the European Commission fined a Swiss Pharmaceuticals company a huge amount of Euros for operating a scheme offering fidelity rebates in connection with drug supplies to pharmacies."

"So you are telling me, Lawrence, that this idea is also a no-go."

"Most definitely, Chairman," responded Lawrence.

"Well, I have to say that I find all of this bureaucracy, together with these ridiculous rules and regulations, very tedious. Everything was so much simpler when doing business after the war. It is a miracle that we can do anything at all nowadays!"

"Oh, sorry, I have just remembered that I need to raise one other matter concerning Atlantic Fortress. Reggie has told me that Anglo-Scottish was previously responsible for overhauling their aircraft and that we have now taken over that work."

"Yes, that is correct, Chairman, we are in the process of closing down the former Anglo-Scottish maintenance operations at Gatwick, and we are transferring the work to Heathrow, where we have surplus capacity."

"I believe you also told me, Reggie, that the rates that Anglo-Scottish charged were very low and only a little above cost?" Reggie nodded his head in agreement.

Lawrence continued. "Also correct, but have carried out a costing exercise and the rates will be increased by fifty percent on 1 December."

"I propose that we treble the current rates. They have nowhere else to go. I do not see why we should help a competitor."

"I am afraid I cannot agree to that, Chairman. We might go to sixty percent, but any higher would be unsupportable and unethical. By consolidating overhaul work at Heathrow, we are already achieving considerable cost savings. Also, we have surplus capacity at Heathrow and so most of the additional revenue from the Atlantic Fortress work flows straight through to the bottom line."

Lawrence continued. "If we increase our rates any higher, then Atlantic Fortress does have an option because there is a maintenance facility in Southern Ireland where they could go to, in the short term, whilst setting up their own maintenance base. If that happens, we will lose all of that additional revenue and, in due course, there will be another facility competing against us for third-party overhaul work."

"Are you telling me that you reject this proposal as well?"

"Chairman, I suggest that decisions on third-party overhaul rates are most definitely for the Executive team rather than the Board. So yes, I do reject your proposal. I am prepared to increase the rates by sixty percent, but by nothing more. I suggest that this should be the end of the matter."

Sir John decided to retreat.

"Well, at least you have allowed me one very small win. As it happens, Laughing Boy has been requesting a meeting with me for quite a while now. I really do not want to make his acquaintance; he is not my kind of person. However, Lawrence, if you are showing me the red card on all of what I had previously thought were perfectly acceptable commercial actions, then it seems I should arrange to meet him and to find out what he has in mind."

"Chairman, yes, I am indeed showing you the red card. You know my strong views. I will not sanction anything in any part of the business which is not fully disclosed or in relation to which there are any legal risks. It will catch up with us in the end. It will be most interesting to learn what Tommy Branscombe has to say for himself."

Chapter 23
Tommy Branscombe

Thomas "Tommy" George Branscombe was lounging on a sofa at his small King's Road, Chelsea offices. Tommy had never owned a desk, and certainly not a conference table. He had no intention of doing so because he much preferred business meetings to be informal, with the participants sofa-seated around a coffee table. With a youthful appearance and still under forty years of age, the long-haired and bearded Tommy was clad in his normal attire of a pullover and jeans. For once, he was alone for the morning; all of his team were out of the office, busily working on various ventures.

This day in mid-October 1988 seemed to be one for a few rare moments of reflection. It was just over twenty years since Tommy had been effectively kicked out of Strutt College. Through scrimping and saving, his middle-class parents had struggled to send him to this prestigious Independent school. Their reward had been five distinctly poor GCEs, not including Maths or a Science subject, and a letter from the Head Master stating, in roundabout terms, that Tommy would not be welcome in the sixth form. The school had clearly decided not to jeopardise its ratings in the Independent Schools Examination Results tables any further by pursuing its efforts to improve the academics of the young Branscombe.

Tommy was dimly aware at the time of his parents' disappointment. It was not until as recently as ten years ago that he discovered, what the school had dismally failed to do, that he had severe dyslexia, including difficulties in dealing with numbers. In the late 1960s, failure to navigate the various academic hurdles was considered simply to indicate that you were of below-average intelligence, and that was it. Despite these unpromising beginnings, one certain thing had soon become apparent: Tommy was one of the world's natural entrepreneurs, with the capability to inspire others. Whilst he had nothing else in common with Sir John Cresswell, the one talent which they both shared was to first spot and then to take maximum advantage of a business opportunity.

After leaving school, Tommy used a small legacy to establish a business importing electrical goods. Three years later, he had set up a factory very successfully for producing hi-fi equipment. Tommy had adopted the name "Fortress" for his ventures simply to signify size and permanence, whether this description was merited or not. Despite his supposed lack of mathematical abilities, by the late 1970s, Tommy had become interested in computing and the huge potential future market for Personal Computers. Tommy purchased licences to produce a range of computing devices. They were well-received by the General Public, and they were sold across the UK and into Europe in very large numbers.

Tommy had also become aware of another way to make money, and it was one which involved minimal financial risk. This method was to harness the marketing value of the Fortress brand through the granting of licenses to both budding entrepreneurs and to established businesses. Tommy had then instructed the company's lawyers to file Trade Mark registrations in all business classes, where there were no existing third-party registrations and where there was any likelihood of a licence deal being struck. A queue soon formed of entities, each wishing to attach the Fortress name to their prospective and existing enterprises. Tommy sometimes took an initial equity stake in the underlying businesses, but he was always looking for opportunities to mitigate risk by involving other shareholders and financiers. Soon, in addition to the original Fortress Electricals, there was a range of companies including Fortress Communications, Fortress Entertainment, Fortress Finance and Fortress Fitness.

Not all of Tommy's ventures had been successful. He had allowed himself, in the early 1980s, to be convinced that there was an opportunity in the United Kingdom snack foods market. The market was currently dominated by a few major brands, with retailer own-label products supplying the remainder.

A manufacturer of own-label products had advised Tommy that there was space to introduce a line of Fortress-branded crisps, nuts and other savoury snack products. The supermarket chains had indicated their support, in principle, and considerable investment had been made in Fortress brand marketing and in the expansion of production capacity. The launch had gone well, but it had soon become apparent that the supermarkets were simply using the Fortress-branded products in order to negotiate lower prices from their major branded suppliers. Within two years, Fortress brand volumes had fallen significantly, and it had been necessary to abandon the project. Fortress Group had received some licensing income, but there had been insufficient time for Tommy to withdraw the Group's equity investment, which had to be written off.

Despite these occasional disappointments, Tommy was still undeterred in his search for the next big opportunity. He considered it had arrived, just over four years previously, when Tommy had been approached by a significantly out-of-pocket Manhattan attorney, Charles "Charlie" Herman 11. Sometime previously, Charlie had agreed to work, on a deferred fee basis, on a project to establish a proposed new airline, Atlantic Express. Before Charlie had received a single dollar of his fees, project funding had run out. In the following liquidation, Charlie had managed to secure ownership of the route licences. However, he had nothing else to show for his extensive labours, other than ongoing responsibility for a small group of ex-Laker Airways personnel. This group was working on obtaining the necessary CAA Operator's Licences, and they were costing him a small fortune.

Hitherto, Tommy had never expressed any particular interest in aviation. A distant Aunt had once worked as an Air Stewardess with British Empire Airways, but there was no other association. This new opportunity had seemed rather different from the usual proposals crossing the coffee table. It strongly appealed to his extroverted and outgoing personality. He did not mess with Charlie, telling him that Fortress Group wished to take ownership of and responsibility for the operation. Charlie would stay involved until the necessary CAA licences were obtained. At that point, he would exit completely from the venture with a payment of one million US Dollars. Charlie realised that this was the best offer he was going to receive, and so he promptly agreed.

The first flight of the new Atlantic Fortress Airways was scheduled to take place in early 1984. The fledgling airline had rented a Jumbo jet on a one-year lease from the Boeing Corporation, and it was crewed by three, newly-retired, ex-British International, Jumbo pilots. The flight was a test flight, as part of the final process of obtaining the required CAA Licences. Around a hundred Fortress Group employees were on board, together with the Press. Tommy was leading the celebrations.

Charlie was also present, as a slightly reluctant passenger who was eagerly looking forward to the successful completion of the flight. He had already booked his ticket to New York on the British Empire Airways Subsonic Cruiser later in the week. When would the Brits wake up to the fact that their Empire was mostly a distant memory and that the continued reference to "Empire" was anachronistic in the extreme? The Cruiser service had been running for about eighteen months. Charlie was unconvinced that the premium fare was worth the slightly shorter travel time. On a bad day, the time gained in flight could be easily lost by delays in Immigration or in Baggage collection. However, by the time Charlie took to the air, it was his expectation that his one million US Dollars would be safely deposited in the bank. Paying the extra fare was not likely to be an issue.

Aboard Atlantic Fortress Airways Flight 1, the champagne corks were popping and the music was playing. Then the merriment came to an abrupt halt as there was a very loud bang, with the aircraft lurching to port. Observations from the port windows showed smoke pouring from the outboard engine. The experienced heads on the Flight Deck were relatively unconcerned. There had been a bird strike, which had effectively destroyed the engine. The pilots immediately shut down the ailing engine and, fortunately, the three other engines were functioning normally. In a much more subdued mood, the passengers were safely returned to Gatwick. Tommy and Charlie were left to deal with the issue of a written-off engine. It had not been possible to insure the engine against the risks of accidental damage until the full CAA Licences had been granted.

A spare engine was available, which was fitted overnight, and the test flight was successfully resumed the next day. This time, only the pilots and CAA personnel were on board. All of the requirements were satisfactorily met, and the CAA Licences were granted. Charlie made his flight to New York, as planned, with his bank balance being at heights never before previously achieved or contemplated. Tommy was now in full marketing mode for the commencement of commercial flights from 1 April 1984. However, with an initial loss of £900,000 already showing in the books for the written-off engine, he was only too well aware that civil aviation was a high-risk business.

Over four years had now passed since the commencement of commercial flights. The way ahead had not been easy, and it had been an exciting, but only marginally profitable period for Atlantic Fortress Airways. Sir Freddie Laker, the great British civil aviation pioneer, had been very generous in lending his expertise and experience to the venture. It was his idea to offer a Super Business Class, equivalent to the First Class service of competitor airlines. Other Laker-inspired initiatives included limousine services from home to the departing airport and from the arriving airport to the specified destination in the locality. Also and of particular attraction to middle-ranking executives was the provision of an Economy Class ticket for every Super Business Class ticket purchased. Wives and partners could now be included in the fun.

Tommy put his reflections to one side for the meantime; it was now time for him to make some key decisions concerning the future of Atlantic Fortress. The Airline lacked critical mass. Although it had an increased fleet of five Jumbos, they were all leased, and they were not getting any younger. Replacement and preferably new aircraft were required. The necessary investment would be significant, and the route network would have to be expanded in order to justify such a commitment. Tommy had agonised for many months over the problem. Ideally, he would have liked to follow his normal practice of reducing the Fortress Group's equity investment, but this was not easy in what was a high-risk airline venture. He had eventually settled on two possible solutions.

First would be some kind of tie-up with British International. Along with other players in the Industry, he had witnessed the brutal breakup of Anglo-Scottish earlier in the year. Sir Adrian McClean had been a popular Industry figure, and there was a widespread view that he had been very poorly treated. Sir John Cresswell had a reputation for being a ruthless adversary, but, behind his Establishment pretensions and by his own admission, he was fundamentally just a good old-fashioned rogue. On the other hand, Lord Avonmouth, who had also been involved in the skulduggery around Anglo-Scottish, was a darker character who had evolved into becoming the consummate politician. It was difficult to know how far to trust either of them. However, some kind of closer relationship with British International was one possible way forward, but a full takeover of Atlantic Fortress Airways was most certainly not on the table.

The second option was for Atlantic Fortress to go it alone. Because of the high level of volatility associated with airlines, Fortress Group would, itself, need to finance the next stage of development of Atlantic Fortress Airways. Specifically, the very large cost of expanding and modernising the airliner fleet. Tommy had reluctantly concluded that the required funds could only be raised by the Fortress Group through the sale of Fortress Electricals. This was his original business and had once been the heart of the Fortress Group. It had become less central in recent years as the Group had expanded, but it was still a large operation. The Personal Computer business was flourishing, and a major recent push had been made into the rapidly expanding market for mobile phones. There was currently a substantial offer on the table for the acquisition of Fortress Electricals by the American-owned Global Electricals. Tommy had been holding them off for some time.

Tommy really did not want to sell Fortress Electricals, and so he had decided to explore option one first. Accordingly, he had picked up the phone to British International, and he had eventually secured a slot in Sir John Cresswell's apparently crammed diary. The meeting would be taking place in the first week of November at the newly-opened, swish office block in Buckingham Gate, where he understood Sir John had a serviced office.

Chapter 24
Sounding Out

The Buckingham Gate Reception desk had phoned through to Sir John advising that a gentleman, announcing himself as Tommy Branscombe, had arrived. Sir John had confirmed that he was expected and that he would meet Mr Branscombe at the lift. He had deliberately not advised Sir Lawrence Marshfield of this meeting, since this was just the early stages, and he wanted to sound out Branscombe alone.

"Good morning, Mr Branscombe, I have been so looking forward to our meeting. Please follow me, the office is just here on the right."

Well, at least Laughing Boy was wearing a jacket today, thought Sir John, although he could see the customary pullover beneath. He might even be wearing slacks rather than jeans. But the hair and beard were as unruly as Sir John had unfortunately expected. In his opinion, they were both in dire need of a barber's attention.

"Please sit down," said Sir John, pointing to the chair in front of his desk, "Coffee is on its way."

"Please call me Tommy, and do you mind if we sit here?" Said Tommy, pointing to the small coffee table on the left of the room with its two low-level chairs. "I think that informal chats are so much more productive, don't you agree, Sir John?"

Sir John certainly did not agree at all, but he said nothing and descended gingerly into one of the low-level chairs. He had never used them for meetings before, and they were certainly not designed for people with back problems.

"Tommy, I'm so sorry it has taken us this long to get together, but as you will appreciate, it has been a very busy few months for us at British International. Now, how may I help you?"

"Sir John, I am equally pleased to have this opportunity. I have admired your many achievements from afar, not least the recent flotation of British International. It is a privilege to be able to meet you in person at last."

Sir John thought to himself. Such an empty compliment and so typical of a brat like you, with your spoilt and privileged middle-class, Public School background. If you believe that you can charm me, Laughing Boy, then you are very much mistaken.

Tommy continued. "Before we start, I should like to thank you very much, Sir John, for taking such a constructive approach to our fleet maintenance requirements. You potentially had us over a barrel, but the arrangement we came to with British International, I think, was a good deal for both parties. If we had not been able to reach an agreement, we were poised to set up our own overhaul facility at Gatwick."

"Thank you for that, Tommy. My colleagues and I were determined not to be seen to be exploiting the situation in any way, and we were delighted to be able to help out. We always try to be very fair in our business dealings. Please now proceed."

"I will come straight to the point, Sir John. As you know, Atlantic Fortress Airways is expanding rapidly. My colleagues and I have concluded that there could be advantages for civil aviation in the United Kingdom if there was some degree of cooperation between its two major international airlines. Rather than knocking seven bells out of each other, we consider that we could work productively together in the best interests of the Nation."

"If I may stop you there for a moment, Tommy. We are very hot on Competition Law here at British International. We would absolutely not engage in any kind of relationship or practice that might be considered as market sharing and thereby potentially an infringement of the law."

"I entirely agree, Sir John and I can assure you that anything that we might propose would be open and clear. No arrangements would be pursued which did not have full Regulatory and Government approvals. May I continue?"

"It is good to hear that, by all means, please carry on."

"Atlantic Fortress is in the process of renewing its fleet and expanding its network. British International has inherited quite a number of unused routes and airport slots from Anglo-Scottish. We believe that an expanded Atlantic Fortress Airways could make good use of these routes and slots and thereby provide more competitive and wider services for the British Public. In addition, we consider that there is potentially a major opportunity for us to work together in establishing a new low-cost short and medium-haul carrier servicing European destinations and which would be based at Gatwick."

"This seems quite an interesting proposition in principle, Tommy. On the low-cost airline aspect, British International is, of course, aware of a small Irish airline which already purports to be a low-cost carrier. I can see some merit in establishing a similar style operation in order to deal with them. What exactly are you suggesting?"

The crunch point had been reached.

"My proposal, Sir John, is that British International should acquire a twenty-five percent shareholding in Atlantic Fortress Airways. We would use these funds for fleet renewal and expansion. British International would transfer its unused routes and airport slots to Atlantic Fortress. We would then activate these routes and utilise the vacant slots to introduce services to be carried out by our expanded fleet. In addition, we would establish a jointly-owned low-cost airline based at Gatwick. British International would allocate some of its surplus Boeing 737 fleet to the new airline, and Atlantic Fortress would have the management and operational responsibility for the new entity. What do you think?"

Sir John was thinking that he had succeeded in flushing out Branscombe without very much difficulty at all. He now knew exactly where he was coming from. Branscombe's arrogance and apparent naivety had been most helpful. British International might now, once and for all, be able to remove the irritation of Atlantic Fortress Airways.

"Well, Tommy, I think this has been a most helpful discussion. As I am sure you will appreciate, there is much to consider with my senior colleagues. All I can say to you at present is that we will give your proposals our very active and close consideration. What is your timescale?"

"Thank you, Sir John, I am really enthusiastic that we will be able to work very well together. As you would expect, we are also evaluating other options, so I really need to hear from you whether it is go or no go by the early part of January next year."

"Tommy, I will make my very best endeavours to get back to you with some thoughts by that time. Unless there is anything else, I suggest we close the meeting and get to work."

Sir John levered himself out of the low chair and escorted Tommy back to the lift. Momentarily, his back pains had taken second place. His Chess brain was actively processing the information which he had just received. He was already in full plotting mode, and a future strategy was being evolved.

Tommy emerged from the serviced offices and onto Buckingham Gate. He was uncharacteristically worried. He had a nagging feeling that he had just volunteered far too much information.

Chapter 25
An Act of Folly

In the first week of December 1988, the dark mornings and dismal weather had closed in, and Sir John had not enjoyed the chauffeured drive out from Belgravia to Hounslow along the M4. Ludicrously, the motorway had been blocked in both directions. The British disease of trying to get a quart into a pint pot was very evident. He had finally arrived at the British International Headquarters, half an hour behind schedule, and he was now convened with Lawrence and Reggie in the Chairman's office.

"Good morning, Chairman. I understand that you had a meeting with Tommy Branscombe a few weeks ago. I'm a little surprised that you did not ask me to accompany you."

"Lawrence, it was only a 'get to know you' kind of chat. I certainly did not need a chaperone. Anyway, it was just a general update with nothing of consequence, although Laughing Boy was very complimentary about our decision to continue with the maintenance of Atlantic Fortress's Jumbos."

Lawrence said nothing, although Reggie knew exactly what he was thinking. All three around the table were fully aware that the agreement to continue maintenance for Atlantic Fortress Airways' aircraft, on reasonable financial terms, had been solely a Lawrence decision, which had been taken in contradiction to the Chairman's suggestion.

"I should mention that Branscombe floated a proposal that we should take a stake in his airline. However, I made it clear that we could not possibly consider such an idea so soon after the flotation. Another matter we touched on was low-cost air travel. Branscombe mentioned that small Irish carrier, which it seems is becoming a bit of a nuisance. What do you know about them?"

"Chairman, you say a small carrier, but it is in fact growing at a very rapid pace. It is Irish registered, but it operates predominantly from and within the UK. It has the most efficient aircraft available, and it uses the lowest cost airports, sometimes a considerable distance from their advertised destinations. There are absolutely no frills. No in-flight meals and everything else, including passenger luggage, is chargeable except for a small carry-on bag."

Sir John responded.

"I am of the opinion, Lawrence, that these low-cost carriers are another potential threat to us. I have been giving some thought to the matter, and I have another proposal to make. I hope you will not dismiss this idea in a similar fashion to the proposals which I made concerning Atlantic Fortress. I still feel you were being rather obstructive at that time and that my previous ideas were mostly quite sensible and reasonable."

"Of course, Sir John, Reggie and I are most interested to hear your latest proposal. Please let us know what you have in mind."

"It's quite simple, really. It's essentially a case of, if you can't beat them, join them. It seems to me that we will soon have a growing number of surplus Boeing 737s, as more new A320s arrive. Rather than selling off these redundant aircraft, sometimes to potential competitors, I believe that we should transfer them from Heathrow and use them to establish our own in-house low-cost carrier based at Gatwick. We will then be very well-positioned to beat the Irish airline and other infiltrators at their own game. What do you think?"

Lawrence drew breath.

"I entirely agree, Chairman, that we need to be mindful of the low-cost threat. However, I am not convinced that setting up our own low-cost operation is the appropriate course of action. It would only serve to divert traffic from our full-service offering. On many routes, we could be effectively competing against ourselves and potentially undermining the viability of our existing operations."

Sir John responded. "I really think you are being over-cautious again. What ideas do you have for dealing with this low-cost threat?"

"Simply that we continue our current efforts to reduce operating costs and to create efficiencies throughout British International. By following this line of action, we can keep our fares low and competitive. If we are still under pressure, then we will have to look at making changes to our full-service offering until we have reduced our cost base sufficiently to match the competition."

Lawrence's reply had slightly deflated Sir John, but he was not going to give up this time. He was convinced that this idea, which he had of course pinched from Tommy Branscombe, was his last chance to put his name to a major growth initiative for British International.

"Lawrence, I hear what you say, but I do see the issue of dealing with the low-cost threat as being a strategic rather than an operational matter. This being the case, I believe that the Board should be fully involved. So I suggest that this topic be added to the Agenda for the January Board meeting."

"I agree that this Agenda addition would be appropriate, Sir John," said Lawrence. "Of course, I will implement whatever decision the Board subsequently decides to make."

Lawrence was pretty sure that setting up a low-cost operation would be a mistake. But he might be wrong, and it was quite clear that Sir John was resolute that the matter should go to the Board for decision.

Chapter 26
Tommy Reacts

At the January 1989 British International Board meeting, there was an extensive debate on the low-cost airline proposal. Lawrence had repeated his concerns and his view that the investment required to establish a low-cost airline would be much better employed in improving efficiencies in the existing mainstream operations of British International. It was apparent, however, that Sir John had been lobbying hard, and eventually the Board had come down on his side. It had agreed to a one-year low-cost airline trial commencing on 1 April 1989.

The new low-cost subsidiary was to be known as "BI Economy" and would be based at Gatwick. Ten British International Boeing 737 aircraft would be re-liveried and allocated to the venture. There would be considerable investment required in crew training and new ticketing systems, and the operation would have its own separate management team. The Board authorised an expenditure of £50 million to set the new airline on its way. Lawrence accepted the turn of events, but he was concerned about viability. He certainly did not favour the name which had been chosen for the new operation. To Lawrence, it might be taken to imply that the mainstream operations of British International were not being run economically!

Back down on the King's Road, Chelsea, Tommy had waited in vain for the promised January response from Sir John. He was about to resume his attempts to make telephone contact when the morning mail arrived. It included the latest issue of Aviation News. The headline was "British International tackles low-cost carriers with new subsidiary". The related article then included a quote from Sir John. The quote stated that the creation of this subsidiary was his personal initiative in order to ensure that British International was a participant in this emerging market sector and that the airline was competitive across all areas of the rapidly developing civil aviation scene.

It took a lot to change Tommy's normal laid-back manner, but what he had read had really made his blood boil. "His personal initiative", indeed, what utter nonsense and blatantly untrue. Sir John had stolen the idea that Tommy had presented to him during their last November meeting. Tommy resolved not to pursue his attempts any further to make telephone contact with Sir John. His next telephone call would be to Global Electricals.

Two months later, the March 1989 issue of Aviation News had carried another interesting headline, "Founder sells business to expand Atlantic Fortress." The related article then included an interview with Tommy Branscombe, who had explained that he had needed to make an agonising choice between his airline and his original Electricals business. He had decided that he loved the airline more. Global Electricals had acquired Fortress Electricals for a staggering £375 million. It was Branscombe's intention to invest most of this very substantial amount in the further development of Atlantic Fortress Airways.

A most important step in this development had already been taken. Tommy had had a very busy few months during which he had taken advantage of a weak market for long-haul aircraft, due to political uncertainties and volatile oil prices. An order for five of the new state-of-the-art Boeing 747-400 series Jumbo jets had been placed. Tommy had negotiated hard, and Boeing had agreed, for a nominal additional price, to install flat screens on seat backs in all of the new aircraft and in all seating classes. These seat back screens were a relatively new concept, but with the benefits of the top-class offerings from Fortress Entertainment, Atlantic Fortress Airways would be offering an even more attractive package to prospective passengers.

Aviation News was also circulating at British International. Lawrence realised that the Airline now had a real fight on its hands. Sir

John had, strangely, gone rather quiet. Reggie continued to be very supportive in all aspects of the business, but he had confirmed to Lawrence that he would be retiring, as planned, early in 1990. BI Economy had seen a reasonably successful launch, but the Irish carrier had retaliated immediately by reducing its fares to even lower levels. BI Economy had been forced to follow.

As the year progressed, Lawrence's prediction that business would be diverted from the full-service operations of British International was proving to be uncomfortably correct. In aggregate, the Airline was carrying more passengers overall, but profit margins had fallen as passengers had moved from its full-service flights to those of BI Economy, where the low-cost carrier was operating on the same routes. BI Economy's fares had been driven far below cost levels due to the competitive responses of the Irish carrier. It was all becoming a rather unpleasant affair.

Chapter 27
A Serious Failure

The January 1990 Board meeting of British International Airlines had been a much more difficult event for Sir John than had been the conduct of business at the previous year's January meeting. The long-haul operations were increasingly suffering from the impact of the new Jumbos, which were now entering service with Atlantic Fortress Airways. Branscombe's rapidly expanding operation was now also flying to the West Coast of America. However, the most serious issue was the state of the short and medium-haul business, where overall profitability was seriously below budget. Profits and passenger numbers in the full-service operation were down, and the introduction of BI Economy was proving to be an unmitigated financial disaster.

Lawrence was tempted to say "I told you so," but clearly restrained himself. The question was what to do now? The required solution was, unfortunately, quite obvious. The one-year trial of BI Economy would not be continued beyond 31 March 1990. Lawrence was instructed to effect the closure of the business as efficiently as possible and to dispose of the assets. The proceeds would be invested in retrofitting seat back screens into the British International long-haul fleet. This action was considered to be essential in order to remain competitive with Atlantic Fortress. The whole BI Economy experiment had been a most unfortunate affair, and no one in British International and particularly Sir John, had been shown in a good light.

It was now mid-April 1990, and Sir John's visits to the Hounslow offices had become less frequent following Reggie's retirement. Today, Lawrence had requested a special meeting with Sir John at the offices.

"Good morning, Sir John, thank you for coming in."

"Nice to see you, Lawrence, and so how is that wonderful wife of yours and the children?"

"All is well at home, thank you, Chairman, but I am getting a bit of stick because of early mornings and late nights. The last few months have been rather tough. I am glad that you were able to come in because I need to have a word with you about BI Economy."

"I thought that episode was all past history."

"Well, BI Economy operations have ceased, and we are now commencing the tidying-up exercise. However, to put it frankly, we have received an offer out of the blue from Atlantic Fortress, proposing to take over the operation as a going concern."

"So typical of that unshaven opportunist. How much is Laughing Boy offering?"

"£25 million is on the table."

"Ridiculous and, as I have said, it's just an opportunist punt."

"I hear that, Chairman, but we estimate that the net proceeds from a break-up of BI Economy and from the follow-up liquidation will be less than half of what he is offering."

"Are you telling me we should accept this low-ball offer?"

"I have concluded that there is no other realistic option. Even then, we will still be showing a £25 million loss on the BI Economy project"

It was clear that the discussion was over. It seemed that Laughing Boy would be the only winner from the BI Economy debacle. Sir John reflected, it had been a disappointing twelve months. He feared that matters might yet get a good deal worse.

Chapter 28
The Final Blow

Sir John had been summoned to the Department of Trade and Industry's Old Admiralty offices. It was a month later, in early May 1990. Sir John was attending in order to present his annual summary of the previous year's performance to the President of the Board of Trade. Unfortunately, the position was still held by his adversary, Lord Avonmouth. Like Sir John, his lordship was frustrated with the turn of events. His targeted elevation to the highest office in the land still seemed no closer.

"Good morning, Sir John, so good to see you again. Shall we get on with matters? How have things been going at British International? The Department is, of course, off the hook after the flotation, but we still have our Golden share, and so we need to keep a close tab on things."

"Good morning, your lordship and I so much appreciate the opportunity to present these annual updates. 1989 was another successful year for British International Airlines. Our excellent Chief Executive Officer, Sir Lawrence Marshfield, whom I selected just over four years ago, continues to provide strong leadership. Fleet modernisation is progressing well and efficiency improvements are being delivered throughout the business."

"Very pleasing to hear that, Sir John; however, I notice you have made no mention of the BI Economy affair."

"Yes, that was a most disappointing outcome. It was an initiative that the Board was determined to pursue. The CEO and I had our reservations about it, but in the end, the Board authorised a one-year experiment, which proved to be unsuccessful."

Not quite the way I have heard it, his lordship thought to himself.

"Thank you, Sir John. I have some updates of my own if you have a few minutes."

"I am entirely at your disposal, your lordship. I have no other engagements this morning."

There was an evil glint in the eyes of his lordship. He was going to enjoy the next few minutes.

"Excellent, the first thing concerns the London Air Traffic Distribution Rules. I think we touched upon this subject at our key flotation meeting back in early 1988, when we discussed the situation of Anglo-Scottish. I recollect your comment at the time that the Government's then long-standing policy for a Second Force Private Sector airline was long outdated. The Government has formed a similar view towards the Rules. Gatwick Airport is now very well established and so we consider it no longer needs these legislative protections. Accordingly, the Rules are to be abolished in July. We have consequently advised Atlantic Fortress Airways that, in addition to its services from Gatwick, it may commence operations from Heathrow later this year."

"I must protest your lordship, any such services from Heathrow will be in direct competition with those of British International." Spluttered Sir John. "Any change in the status quo will significantly undermine our operations."

"Sir John, the Government wishes, in future, to encourage a free and open market in civil aviation. It no longer has any direct involvement or financial interest in the sector, as was previously the case when the Government owned British International. The Airline must now stand on its own two feet. Large sums were extracted from the Treasury in order to fund redundancy and pensions costs, not to mention the scandalously low price which was extorted for British International to acquire the Subsonic Cruiser fleet. I should also mention that the Government will be cancelling all those British

International route licences which are currently unused. These routes will be put up for auction. As a consequence, British International will be obliged to relinquish ownership of the associated airport slots."

"But taking away those routes and airport slots is an act which amounts to nothing less than a confiscation of British International Airlines' property." Fumed Sir John.

Warming to his task, Lord Avonmouth responded with a barely disguised smirk on his face.

"I think not. As I said a moment ago, the Government wishes to encourage open competition in civil aviation and, where route and airport slots are not being used, we consider ourselves obliged to make them available to other suitable operators. Atlantic Fortress Airways would certainly meet our criteria in this regard."

Sir John inwardly groaned. It seemed he was not going to win in this conversation. All of this bad news was clearly a part of getting your own back and in spades. He made a final attempt to salvage something from the situation, hoping that no further blows would rain down from his lordship.

"Your lordship, I consider this is a very extreme position to take and so shortly after the flotation. If these changes are pursued, then they will crash the British International share price."

"So be it, there is plenty of time for the share price and for the Airline to recover. As you yourself have said, Sir John, it is under excellent management. I have every confidence that management will rise to the challenge. There is just one further item before we finish."

This last stage of the meeting was something which Sir John had both been looking forward to and also dreading. But, deep down, he already knew what was about to transpire.

The glint in his lordship's eyes had turned icy.

"As you know, Sir John, the Government still retains a Golden share in British International Airlines, which conveys the right, for the meantime, to appoint the Chairman. I am aware that your initial term finishes at the end of this month. I regret to inform you that your appointment is not to be extended for a further term. However, we do wish you to stay on until the end of August. This will enable you to preside over the Annual General Meeting and to receive appropriate appreciation for your excellent stewardship of British International over the past five years."

Lord Avonmouth continued.

"I must say that this decision has been made solely having regard to the new Corporate Governance Standards, now being more widely observed in the private sector. They provide that directors should generally retire at age seventy. I believe that you will soon be seventy-three, but you certainly do not look it. The Government feels obliged to follow these emerging trends from the private sector when making or extending appointments to current or former public sector entities. The Prime Minister has been consulted and he has concurred with this decision. However, I am delighted to tell you that he has agreed with my suggestion that you should be offered the position of Honorary President of British International Airlines plc."

The bad news had been delivered, and the Prime Minister had clearly been nobbled. The fortunes of British International had been damaged, at least in the short term. Sir John's long-held ambitions and hopes to see out his career as the continuing Chairman of a high-profile and growing business, and with the associated emoluments, had also just been dashed. It was not correct for Lord Avonmouth to say that these so-called emerging trends from the private sector were being widely followed. They had certainly not been applied when the Government had made many other contemporary senior appointments.

Sir John decided quickly that he would not be peevish and that he would accept the short-term extension of office to the end of August. Such an extension would enable him to make the Annual General Meeting his last public platform. At a time of his choosing, he would decline the offer of the Honorary Presidency. It was a completely meaningless gesture and more akin to an insult.

Chapter 29
The Retaliation

The British International Airlines plc 1990 Annual General Meeting was held in August at the splendid building in London's Pall Mall, which accommodated the offices and dining facilities of the Institute of Directors. Amongst those in attendance, in his capacity for the purposes of this event as a British International shareholder, was Sir Adrian McClean. He was now midway through his Chairmanship of the Institute, which he was much enjoying. Reggie Laycock was also in the audience, now fully retired from his executive duties as Company Secretary, but still managing the Final Salary Pension Scheme and keeping a close eye on matters generally. There was no sign of Lord Avonmouth or of anyone else from the Department of Trade and Industry, although members of the Press were strongly in evidence.

Sir John was on the platform with Lawrence to his right and, to his left, was the lawyer, aged in his mid-forties, who had been recruited as Reggie's replacement. The formal business was satisfactorily completed. There were then a number of speeches from the floor in appreciation of Sir John's service to the company, and Sir John gratefully acknowledged the kind words.

"It has been a privilege indeed to have been involved with British International. It has been a turbulent five years, and so much has been achieved, not least through the efforts of our outstanding Chief Executive Officer, Sir Lawrence Marshfield. Before I bring the meeting to a close, there is, however, just one more important announcement to make."

Lawrence exchanged quick looks with the new Company Secretary. They were mystified; so far as they were both concerned, the business of the meeting was over, and there was nothing further to add.

Sir John rose up to his full and most imposing height.

"Shareholders will be aware that your company has previously made quite substantial donations to the Conservative Party. Your Board has reviewed this practice and has determined that it is inappropriate to favour any particular political party. Further, that there should be no political donations in the future to any party. The Board has resolved, therefore, that the amount of £250,000, which has previously been donated to politics, should be applied elsewhere. In the place of any future political donations, the Board has decided to make a payment of £125,000 per annum to the British International Airlines Benevolent Fund. A further £125.000 will be utilised each year to benefit young people by providing additional spaces in the British International Airlines Apprentices Scheme. Although shareholders are not required to vote on this matter, I very much hope that they will be supportive."

There was spontaneous applause from the floor. Sir Adrian was the leader of the appreciative audience. He had always tried to look after his employees in the past, and Sir John's proposal could not be faulted. Reggie was beaming broadly and amused to observe the obvious discomfort of his procedure-driven younger successor. The Press was scribbling energetically. For a leading British company to cease political donations in this manner, especially having made them previously to the current governing party, was headline news.

The new Company Secretary was frantically trying to catch his eye, but Lawrence declined to engage. Lawrence laughed to himself. There had never been a Board discussion on the policy concerning political donations, but the genie was now out of the bottle. The retiring Chairman had made an announcement in a public forum, which had been loudly applauded by shareholders and which was about to be widely reported. These proposed alternative uses of the funds formerly used for political donations were commendable and could not possibly be criticised. There was absolutely nothing that the Government or the

Conservative Party could now do about it. There was no going back! Well done, Chairman, every dog has his day, and today was yours.

Chapter 30
Full Circle?

It was a beautiful sunny day at Bishop's Lake in the autumn of 1990. The surrounding trees were resplendent in their rustic glow as they prepared for the winter ahead. As was his habit, each day when he was at Bishop's Lake, Sir John had lumbered up the short walk from the house to the top of the mound.

He was still chortling over a letter he had received, shortly after the British International Airlines Annual General Meeting, from Lord Avonmouth, deploring his breach of Corporate Governance Standards by making an announcement at the meeting which had not been subject to the required vetting and approvals procedures. Sir John had been inclined to deposit the letter in the waste bin, but had decided to keep it as part of his archives. You never know, people might be interested in the events of recent years; someone might even decide to write about them in the future.

The BMW 7 Series had now been returned to the British International car pool, where he understood that Gerry was still holding his own. There was a middle-aged Land Rover garaged at Bishop's Lake, but it was suitable only for local trips. For what were now becoming just occasional visits to London, Sir John had acquired a late 1950s Rolls-Royce Silver Cloud. This was similar to the car that he and Laura had so enjoyed together when the Midlands & West Group had really taken off in the late 1950s. The car had strong, robust seats which supported his back well.

Sir John was enjoying the novelty of driving himself once more, having been chauffeured around for so many years. He also liked tinkering with the engine. This was something which you could not do with a modern car, and the tinkering took him back many years to his pre-war days at West London Motors. The Silver Cloud was from an era when Rolls-Royce was the undisputed maker of the best cars in the world. Although its heating and ventilation capabilities were not to modern standards and so not entirely to Eleanor's exacting liking, she was content that she was, at least, still travelling in a Rolls-Royce.

It was the occasion of Sir John's seventy-third birthday. There had been some items in the post. Miss Palmer had sent a card and a note with her best wishes, trusting that he and Lady Eleanor were in good health. She was now a member of the Barking Computer Appreciation Society. The membership records of both the Historical Society and the Book Club had been computerised, and she was producing regular newsletters. Miss Palmer's bowling activities were also going well, and she was first reserve for the Essex Senior Lawn Bowls Team.

She had also been in touch with Harry Shining, who sent his best wishes and who had asked to be remembered. Harry was happily working, part-time, at the Hove B&Q Do It Yourself store, lending his expertise, whether requested or not, in assisting customers to select the tools and materials required for their various projects.

A parcel had also been received. It comprised a box of his favourite finest Havana cigars, one of which was now resting in his breast pocket. Accompanying the box was a note. The letterhead indicated that it was from "The Chairman's Office, British International Airlines plc" and the note read: "Dear Sir John, Wishing you a happy birthday and best wishes for the future. Lawrence."

Sir John lit his cigar and seated himself on the bench situated between the occupied and vacant plots. Now that the hurly burly of the last few months had subsided, he had been able to review his finances over the weekend. Something which he had neither needed nor bothered to do for many years. The results of the review were not encouraging. The non-renewal of his term of office at British International had resulted in the loss of his Chairman's fees and emoluments. He had then been disconcerted to find, ridiculously, that his only secure source of ongoing regular income was the lowly Basic State Pension.

He had never been a member of a company-sponsored pension scheme. It was standard practice for directors not to join the pension schemes of the companies where they served as Officers. He had ensured the protection of the pension benefits of the older, long-service employees during the takeover of the Midlands & West Group. This action had been much appreciated by the beneficiaries, including Jennifer Palmer and Harry Shining. Ironically, the result was that they now both had secure annual retirement incomes which were significantly higher than that of their former Chairman!

Further, most of Sir John's capital assets had been transferred to the Cresswell Family Investment Company many years ago, for Inheritance Tax saving purposes. Although Sir John had a deciding vote over the affairs of the Investment Company, he could neither personally access any of these assets nor draw any income. Of course, he still had the Bishop's Lake Estate, and he would now need to address himself very seriously to making the Estate's 500 acres work very much harder in order to become more economically viable. The low productivity of the Estate was something else which had not hitherto been a concern.

There were a few other investments, including the shares which had been allotted to him in the British International flotation. However, he would not be receiving any more share allotments. Further, the value of his current British International holding had fallen significantly, following the Government's actions to open up Heathrow and to take away routes and airport slots. To sell his British International shares now, at their current depressed value, would be far too soon after the flotation. However, his annual income situation would probably make some early sales necessary, unless some other solution to provide an adequate future income could be found.

He had deliberately left his BlackBerry at the house. There were not many calls nowadays; those that were received were usually from

Eleanor. Much to her annoyance, Reggie's replacement as the British International Airlines' Company Secretary had been quick to exercise the break clause in the lease of the Belgravia apartment, which would now terminate at the end of October. Eleanor had discovered, from her friend Fiona, who was engaged in a messy divorce and still working at the Estate Agency, that the apartment opposite, which had served as a temporary refuge after the 1987 fire incident, would be becoming vacant and potentially for sale at around that time.

There had then been a further clash with the new Company Secretary, who had informed Eleanor that the Desmond Pollock-acquired furnishings should not be moved to any proposed replacement property. These items were owned by British International, and they would be auctioned. If her ladyship wished to participate in the auction, then she was welcome to do so. At this very trying time, Eleanor had once again reached out to Desmond Pollock, who had said that he would be delighted to support her ladyship once again through a very unfair second eviction.

Sir John decided he would return Eleanor's calls later. She would be absolutely furious to hear that the dire financial situation would mean no question of being able to fund a replacement London property. There would be no insurance claim this time, and the awful Desmond Pollock would certainly not be receiving another juicy commission. Unless Eleanor was prepared to dip into her small amount of personal capital, and she had never previously shown any inclination to do so, she would not be a participant in the forthcoming furniture auction.

They would do well just to hang on to Bishop's Lake, and they would certainly need to cut back on staff. Eleanor's monthly allowance from the Cresswell Family Investment Company, which had previously been applied by her to fund her social programme at the Belgravia apartment, would now be required to help with their basic living requirements at Bishop's Lake. Eleanor would have to confine her future social aspirations to the County set. At least she had succeeded in her attempt to become a Deputy Lieutenant of the County.

Sir John looked upwards as an airliner passed overhead. It was climbing away from the nearby Birmingham Airport, and the orange-coloured engine nacelles and the stylised "F" on the tail clearly identified it as being one of the Atlantic Fortress Airway's fleet. It was possibly one of the Boeing 737s previously operated by the defunct BI Economy and which was now flying with the low-cost Division of Atlantic Fortress.

Sir John thought to himself, "So what next, Laughing Boy? Maybe space travel?"

"Sorry to ignore you for a moment, Laura my love. You have never objected to my little indulgence, although I do agree it is rather early in the day for cigars. I seem to be in a bit of a financial spot. You would never have allowed me to take my eye off the ball at Midlands & West Group and to allow that crafty Hansard character to destroy our hard work."

"We might now be facing the necessity to sell Bishop's Lake, and I could well be taking up cooking again. I so remember those happy times in the past when the children were safely in bed and I prepared our Sunday evening steak dinners. It was so good to be able to enjoy the simple dish together and to indulge in a modest bottle of wine."

"It seems that playing airline games might have been a bad mistake. I should have been content with what we had achieved together; the other grass was clearly not greener, after all. I have even resigned from Whites. The contacts there are no longer of much use, and I cannot really afford the subscriptions any more. Maybe where we have arrived at today is just a simple case of us coming full circle? Well, if it is such a situation, then so be it, but it's been one hell of a ride along the way!"

"I will be going fishing in a few minutes, Laura. The old back does not take too kindly nowadays to the recoil of the guns. Anyway, we seem to be out of favour with the shooting community. Not many people are accepting our invitations for shooting weekends any more. So I think I may be closing the lodge quite soon."

"Will speak with you again tomorrow, my love, at the usual time."

Sir John rose slowly from the bench and walked steadily in the direction of the fishing lake. The financial future for Lady Eleanor and himself was currently uncertain, but Sir John was not to be beaten. He was not a quitter and life would go on. He was an optimist. Time would tell if the unexpected might yet turn up.

www.ingramcontent.com/pod-product-compliance
Lightning Source LLC
Chambersburg PA
CBHW071752120626
46550CB00002B/757